LOST ARROWHEADS AND BROKEN POTTERY

LOST ARROWHEADS AND BROKEN POTTERY

A HISTORY OF NATIVE AMERICANS IN BEAR MOUNTAIN STATE PARK, NEW YORK

EDWARD J. LENIK

Purple Mountain Press
FLEISCHMANNS, NEW YORK

Palisades Interstate Park Commission Press
BEAR MOUNTAIN, NEW YORK

Published by
Palisades Interstate Park Commission
Administration Building
3006 Seven Lakes Drive
Bear Mountain, NY 10911
845-786-2701, 845-786-1784 (fax)
www.palisadesparksconservancy.org

Purple Mountain Press, Ltd.
P.O. Box 309
Fleischmanns, New York 12430
845-254-4062, 845-254-4476 (fax), purple@catskill.net
www.catskill.net/purple

Printed in the United States of America.
Cover illustration: A typical rockshelter within Harriman State Park
in the Hudson Highlands, 2000. Photograph by Edward J. Lenik.

ISBN-13 978-0-916346-82-9 ISBN 0-916346-82-X
Library of Congress Control Number: 2009937700

First printing
Manufactured in the United States of America on acid-free paper

TO JACK FOCHT,

director emeritus, Trailside Museums,

fellow explorer, conservationist,

and friend

CONTENTS

ILLUSTRATIONS

FIGURES

TABLES

ACKNOWLEDGMENTS

This monograph is a monument to the exceptional interest, persistence, and active search for information about the prehistory and history of Palisades Interstate Park by Jack Focht, director emeritus of Trailside Museums & Zoo.

I thank my colleagues Tom Fitzpatrick and Nancy Gibbs for their indispensable help in locating and documenting the archaeological sites in Bear Mountain and Harriman state parks. I offer special thanks to the Student Conservation Association's archaeological interns at Trailside: Ed Whritner ('00), Aaron Ziemann ('01), Niall Cytryn ('02), Rachel Cohen-Stevens ('03), Matt Shook ('04-'05), Michelle Houser ('06), Kelly Foxworthy ('07), Charlee Eaton ('08), and Arianna Drumond ('09). I'm especially grateful to Val Cutajar of the Thendara Club and John G. McCullough for coordinating the many dedicated volunteers who monitor the sites. My thanks also to Edwin McGowan, PIPC Press administrator; Jeanne E. Ross, PIPC's editor; Barbara Thomas, Elayne Keith-Feller, Erica Nagel, and Michelle Riley, PIPC facilitators; and Cindy LaBreacht, designer.

Lois Feister, archaeologist with the New York State Bureau of Historic Sites, provided the inventory of all prehistoric artifacts recovered from Fort Montgomery during the 1967–1971 and 2002 excavations. Her cooperation and interest in this study are much appreciated.

Finally, I'm indebted to pioneer archaeologist James D. Burggraf (1911–1994) and his associates at Trailside for conducting archaeological site surveys and excavations in the parks during the 1930s and 1940s. The artifact collections they amassed and their accompanying field notes are important contributions to the archaeology of the Hudson Valley.

Edward J. Lenik
Honorary Curator, Archaeology
Trailside Museums

FIGURE I Seventeenth-century map showing the location of Indian bands in the Hudson River Valley and coastal New York. (Nicholas J. Visscher, 1656)

PROLOGUE

The Hudson River Valley was a good place to live. The Creator had provided generously for the needs of the Indian people. They were thankful and used the land and the waters carefully, sparingly, with good sense. In the river they fished for shad, eel, white perch, black seabass, tomcod, herring, striped bass, and sturgeon. At low tide, they collected softshell clams, mussels, and especially oysters.

The great river divided the land. A canoe in the water or a hunter on a riverside trail could travel to the Hudson's mouth, to the ocean's edge, to the islands and shores, which gave good shelter, to forage the ocean's bounty. Small brooks and creeks provided pathways into the mountains, ridges, and valleys where the forests, marshes, and lakes provided abundant animals and plants necessary for the good life. The Creator provided rock-shelters to camp in, high points to watch from, marshes teeming with game. Deer, bear, beaver, rabbit, turtles, birds were all there, heavy upon the land.

The land grew everything the Indian people needed for a good life. The forest provided wood to make canoes, fires, spears, and bows and arrows, and saplings to frame dwellings. Marsh and forest plants supplied food, medicine, and fibers for mats and baskets. The soil itself gave up clay to make cooking pots and stones from which sharp tools could be fashioned.

The web of trails and river routes etched upon the land mirrored the intricate social and trade networks that linked the people together. Some lived in small bands along the river or streams or in the highland hollows. Some stayed year-round in the larger villages at the river junctions or along the sheltered coasts. Seasonal hunting and gathering opportunities drew them together to work a harvest and celebrate the bounty of the Creator. At these gatherings friendships grew, marriages were arranged, and kinship bonds reinforced the cooperative spirit. People were known by the name of the place they came from. Living groups were led by councils of elders.

The people of the lower Hudson River Valley were Eastern Algonkian speakers of the Munsee and Mahican languages. The Munsee-speakers lived throughout the lower Hudson Valley and the coastal areas of New York and New Jersey. North, along the Hudson River above the Highlands, were the Mahicans. The Unami language was spoken by the Indian people in New Jersey who lived south of the Raritan River and the Delaware Water Gap. Before the coming of Europeans, these three linguistic groups enjoyed relatively peaceful relationships conducive to trade. The Indians of the lower Hudson Valley had no common name for themselves; rather, they referred to themselves as people of this place or that village. The Dutch and their English successors frequently referred to these people collectively as the River Indians. In the seventeenth century, the Dutch identified many Indian settlements along the banks of the Hudson River and in the interior highlands (Figure 1).

The arrival of European settlers disturbed the balance of land use. At first, Indians gave up their hunting areas and joined with others who had room for more people. Rather quickly, the Europeans' demands for land, game, and furs diminished the abundance the Creator had provided.

Few are left of the people who originally occupied this land. We read of them in the journals of the early white explorers, missionaries, and settlers; we follow their retreat and decimation in front of the relentless progress of civilization on the land.

As their land holdings grew smaller, the Indians were caught up in wars with the Europeans and were menaced by the Iroquois. Over time, most sold their lands to the settlers and moved away.

We hear the echoes of their voices in the names of our lakes, rivers, streams, and towns. We see traces of their presence in the patterns of roads and old villages etched upon the land. We walk in their footsteps on the fragments of woodland that we preserve from our civilization. We, too, stop to wonder, to thank the Creator, at the places of singular beauty—these places they marked and named. They are still shadows, memories upon our land.

ARCHAEOLOGY BECOMES
A TRAILSIDE SCIENCE

M ost museum programs usually delight in frogs, snakes, and mugwort, not prehistoric archaeological investigations. Built on the site of the Revolutionary War's Fort Clinton, Trailside Museums & Zoo at Bear Mountain was different from the start. As the dirt was turned during its construction, the site revealed centuries-old features and yielded numerous artifacts. Some of those artifacts were prehistoric Indian items.

Trailside Museums & Zoo was founded in 1927. William H. Carr, its first director, published an account of his work in 1937 in the book *Ten Years of Nature Trailing*. Archaeological field work was part of that story. "We also carried on extensive field work and research in the adjacent counties of Orange and Rockland," Carr wrote. "Mr. James D. Burggraf, Trailside Archeologist, visited and scientifically worked forty-two sites, recovering twenty-five hundred specimens" (Figure 2).

Carr does not point out that this work was even more of an accomplishment than it seems at first: Burggraf became the first full-time archaeologist at the museum in 1935. In his report on his first year on the job Burggraf observed: "This summer, being new to the region, we have concentrated on local sites within the confines of the Palisades Interstate Park, with the result that many specimens of particular interest to the museum have been obtained. Later on definite areas of the surrounding country will be intensely prospected to determine the archaeological resources they possess."

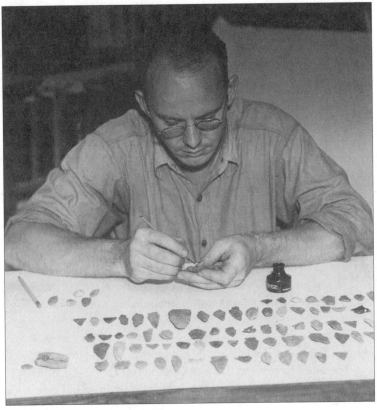

FIGURE 2 James Burggraf numbering and cataloging artifacts at the Trailside Museums in 1941. COURTESY TRAILSIDE MUSEUMS.

Burggraf touches on two purposes that archaeology was to serve at Trailside. First, the Historical Museum needed artifacts for exhibition. Burggraf's job description, dated April 6, 1936, reads: "Maintain, care for, exhibit and collect Indian materials of the Hudson Highlands. Keep study collections and all Indian catalogues and card systems in up-to-date condition. Aid in general historical work, indoors and out, and assist in general preparation work where this is required." Thus, collections were being made for exhibition and for study.

Trailside was interested not in filling cases with Indian artifacts but in interpreting the lives of the Indian groups native to the Hudson Highlands. A May 13, 1936, outline, "Types of Local Indian Exhibits

Needed in Museum," lists six aspects of Indian life the exhibits should address and three additional areas to consider. The theme was "Indian Art and Industries." Models, drawings, material samples, and examples of artifacts illustrate how the Indians lived and made use of the materials nature provided.

Burggraf was designing exhibits even as he was working to understand prehistoric life in this region. That was the second purpose of archaeology at Trailside. There were sites to be discovered and excavated so that the artifacts, features, and stratigraphy—the science of archaeological analysis—could provide data for exhibits and stories for presentation and publication, all of which would expand knowledge and understanding of who lived here.

Trailside had in James Burggraf the perfect man for the job. Born in the Bronx in 1911, he was 25 years old when he became the Museums' archaeologist. His early interest in archaeology focused on Long Island, and his first dig was at the Crab Meadow shell heaps. His training was informal, learned from collectors and pothunters. Burggraf worked in a time when formally trained archaeologists took little interest in local prehistory and instead focused on exotic foreign places. Burggraf was also a skilled illustrator with an eye for detail and a talent for making models of rock-shelters and habitation sites for the exhibits. He remarks in his museum report, "It is seldom that one meets a visitor who knows how an arrow or other chipped stone artifact is worked. It has become standard with me, if explanations fail to convey the idea sufficiently, I bring out a flaking tool of deer antler that I have made and demonstrate on a flint chip."

Burggraf set a high standard in all aspects of his job—locating and digging sites and artifacts, crafting exhibits for the Museums, and taking time with visitors to explain what he knew. He struggled, however, with an unwritten part of the job: to provide exciting finds for the glory of the park. Archaeology, then as now, was expected to be glamorous and its material finds exciting entertainment.

Burggraf worked at Trailside at a time when the prehistory of New York State and northeastern North America was a new research topic. It was exciting to him and others of a scholarly, scientific bent, but it did not produce finds to rival King Tut's tomb.

Dr. William Ritchie of the Rochester Museum, who later became the archaeologist for the State of New York, was constructing his projectile-point typology and interpretation of prehistoric Indian life during these years. Ritchie and Burggraf began a correspondence in 1937 that lasted beyond Burggraf's years at the Museums. In these letters, Burggraf offers Ritchie descriptions, drawings, photographs, and his thoughts on the sites that he and others excavated in the park. Ritchie encourages him to continue to dig and research; Burggraf responds to the encouragement. His letters are studded with interlinear sketches. The men debate the existence of a "Coastal culture" that extended up the Hudson and was more like the cultures of New England than the Iroquois of New York.

Thus, through his discussions with Ritchie and his articles in several historical and archaeological publications, Burggraf's work at Trailside did more than fill museum cases and provide information for exhibit signs. It established archaeology as an important member of the Trailside sciences.

Burggraf was, however, becoming increasingly distressed about providing fodder for the Palisades Interstate Park's publicity machine. He wrote to Ritchie in 1943 that William Carr, "looks at archaeology with the eye of a P. T. Barnum." In later correspondence he acknowledges that Carr was pressured to produce stories for the press. "I wanted to write up everything in cold scientific facts," Burggraf wrote, "but the publicity department wanted wildcat estimates of a hoary antiquity... on some arrowpoint that was likely a transition between Castle Creek, and, for all I could tell, Mid-Victorian!"

Burggraf left Trailside because of World War II. He was called up for the military draft but was offered civilian construction work at the Iona Island Naval Depot, a mile south of Bear Mountain. He told Ritchie, "I decided I could enjoy life more as a free lance 'pot hunter' and get paid twice the wages as a carpenter in the bargain." He spent six days a week building railroad trestles. In his spare time at Iona Island, now part of Bear Mountain State Park, he continued searching for sites, digging and documenting what he found. He maintained his correspondence with Ritchie and this saved correspondence added to the research he left at Bear Mountain.

James Burggraf set the parameters of archaeology at Trailside, and he set them high. Good archaeology has been a part of the Museums ever since. Most of the sites reviewed in this book were located, dug, collected, and documented by Burggraf. The collections are part of Trailside's archives, and members of Trailside's Native American Site Stewardship Program regularly monitor the sites.

CHAPTER 1

INDIAN CULTURE HISTORY

The prehistory of Bear Mountain is presented here as a cultural and dating reference for the discussions of Indian sites that follow. This is a region of diverse topography and environmental settings where many Indian cultures lived and prospered for thousands of years (Figure 3).

The prehistoric archaeological record of the area consists of four time periods of Indian culture history: Paleo Indian, Archaic, Woodland, and Historic Contact. Projectile points and pottery are among the most commonly found artifacts at prehistoric sites and are frequently used as a means of dating them. In the following sections, the principal cultural "markers" of each period are discussed up to and including the point at which a new group of people, the European explorers and settlers, arrived with a new material culture, which included a written language.

PALEO INDIAN PERIOD (CA. 10,500–8000 B.C.)

The Paleo Indian period includes the time from the retreat of the Wisconsin Glacier from the region to the development of modern Holocene environments. Following deglaciation, the landscape consisted of tundra-like vegetation that included sedges, mosses, and lichens. This was succeeded by open parkland vegetation characterized by a mosaic of grasslands and coniferous forests. Initially the climate was wet and cold, but gradual warming took place, resulting in the expansion of boreal forests dominated by spruce and fir.

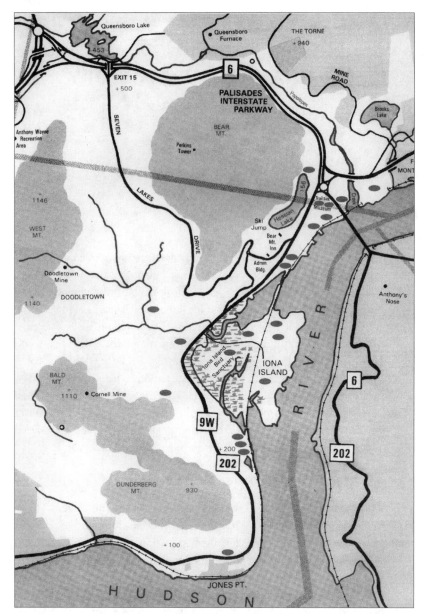

FIGURE 3 Map of Bear Mountain State Park by Robert P. Wallace, with general locations of Indian campsites. Adapted from Trail Map of Bear Mt. & Harriman State Parks, Palisades Interstate Park Commission, Bear Mountain, New York.

Faunal species such as mammoth, mastodon, caribou, giant beaver, elk, moose, peccary, bear, and horse were present in the region and potentially available for exploitation by early Paleo Indian hunters. Many of these animals are now extinct or no longer native to the area.

The Paleo Indians were hunter-gatherers who roamed widely in search of food and raw materials. They traveled in single or multiple family bands, and evidence of their presence in the region has been found. Their settlement pattern consisted of small temporary camps. Archaeologists have identified such sites as occupation-domestic camps, quarries and workshops, caches, bone deposits, and isolated or scattered finds of stone tools. Some of the important Paleo Indian sites in the region are Dutchess Quarry Cave in Orange County, Kings Road and West Athens Hill in the Hudson River Valley, Twin Fields in Ulster County, and Port Mobil on Staten Island.

The material remains of the Paleo Indians primarily includes high-quality stone tools used in the procurement and processing of faunal species and plants, and in the working of bone, wood, and hides. Their tool kits included Clovis-type distinctively fluted spear points, a diagnostic artifact of this period, and bifacial knives, wedges, drills, gravers, burins, scrapers, flake cores, and flake tools with no formal shape.

ARCHAIC PERIOD (CA. 8000–1000 B.C.)

During the Archaic period, a major shift occurred in the settlement and subsistence patterns of Indian groups. Hunting and gathering were still the basic ways of life but the emphasis in subsistence shifted from larger game animals, which were rapidly becoming extinct or unavailable, to smaller game and plants of the deciduous forest. The environment differed from the earlier period as open grasslands disappeared and temperate habitats of oak, hickory, pine, and hemlock forests were established.

The settlement patterns of the Archaic people indicate larger, relatively more permanent habitation sites. These people were very efficient in the exploitation of their environment; plant-food resources, along with fish and shellfish, played a more important role in their diet.

The tool kit of the Early Archaic people (ca. 8000-6000 B.C.) was basically the same as that of the Paleo Indians, with the exception of projectile points. Early Archaic projectile points are bifurcated or basally notched and generally made of high-quality stone. Several Early and

Middle Archaic sites have been found in the lower Hudson River Valley, including Piping Rock, Montrose Point, Dogon Point, Twombly Landing, Parham Ridge, Bannerman Island, and Sylvan Lake.

The Middle Archaic period spans the time between 6000 B.C. and 4000 B.C. The archaeological record suggests that a population increase took place during this period. Corner-notched and stemmed projectile points called Neville, often fashioned from local materials, were prominent. Tool kits of Middle Archaic people also included grinding stones, mortars, and pestles.

During the Late Archaic period (ca. 4000 B.C. to 1000 B.C.), the Indians were more specialized hunter-gatherers who exploited a variety of upland and lowland settings in a well-defined and scheduled seasonal round. Projectile points of this period were diverse and included corner-notched, side-notched, and stemmed types with wide or narrow blades and variable length. Other tools were woodworking implements such as stone axes, adzes, gouges, milling equipment, and netsinkers. Elaborate ceremonialism developed and exotic trade items such as copper adzes and spear points were imported from sources in the upper Midwest. These copper tools have been found in burial sites. Numerous open-air campsites and rockshelters containing Late Archaic components have been found and excavated within Harriman and Bear Mountain state parks.

Toward the end of the Late Archaic period, from about 2000 B.C. to 1000 B.C., new and radically different broad-bladed projectile point types named Susquehanna, Perkiomen, Orient Fishtail, and Koens-Crispin were developed. The use of steatite or stone bowls and the introduction of clay pottery vessels are hallmarks of this era. Archaeologists refer to this time as the Terminal Archaic or Transition period.

WOODLAND PERIOD (CA. 1000 B.C.–A.D. 1600)

The Woodland period is also divided into Early, Middle, and Late time frames. It is distinguished from the Archaic period by the extensive use of ceramic vessels. Horticulture began during this time and became well established with the cultivation of corn, beans, squash, and tobacco. Clay pots replaced soapstone bowls and bows and arrows replaced spears and javelins. Pipe smoking was adopted. The habitation sites of the Woodland-period Indians increased in size and permanence.

The use of fired clay ceramic vessels started during the Early Woodland period (ca. 1000 B.C. to A.D. 1). With the use of ceramics, Indian groups became more sedentary and increased their social complexity over time. Elaborate ceremonialism is evident at a number of burial sites as indicated by the red ochre (a natural pigment), copper beads, effigy figurines, gorgets, pendants, and large stone blades that were interred with the deceased. Copper beads, awls, and tubular stone pipes were imported trade goods from the Midwest. Projectile points, including the Meadowood and Adena types, are also chronological indicators of the Early Woodland-Ceramic period.

During the Middle Woodland period (ca. A.D. 1 to 1000), the use of decorative motifs such as cord marking on ceramic vessels became common. Hunting, fishing, and gathering activities continued on a seasonal cycle. Data from archaeological excavations indicate that Indian groups developed long-distance social, political, and trade networks during this time. Diagnostic projectile points of the Middle Woodland period include types such as Fox Creek and Jack's Reef.

The Late Woodland period spans nearly six centuries, from the end of the Middle period to the arrival of European settlers. Collared ceramic vessels appeared including many with incised decorations. Large triangular projectile points known as the Levanna type became common throughout this period; smaller triangular forms known as Madison emerged near its end. Hunting, fishing, and gathering activities continued, but maize, bean, squash, and pumpkin horticulture became increasingly important in many areas, resulting in the establishment of larger communities or villages.

Palisaded villages developed in some regions during the end of the Late Woodland period. This suggests that episodes of warfare occurred along with cultural and village instability.

HISTORIC CONTACT PERIOD (CA. A.D. 1524–1750)

The first documented contact between Indian people and Europeans in the region occurred in 1524 when Giovanni da Verrazzano sailed into New York Harbor. In 1609, Henry Hudson, an English mariner working for the Dutch, sailed up the river that would ultimately bear his name. Later voyages by the explorers Cornelius May and Adriaen Block resulted in the establishment of the first Dutch trading post at Fort Nassau on the upper Hudson River near Albany in 1614. By 1623, with the settlement of New Amsterdam (New York) by the Dutch, a regular pattern of Indian–European trade developed.

Ethnohistoric evidence indicates that the Indians in this region spoke closely related Eastern Algonkian languages at the time of contact. Indians in central and upstate New York, however, spoke Northern Iroquoian languages. Each ethnic or tribal group had its own distinct dialect, social and political organization, and spiritual beliefs, but all shared to some extent a regional cultural tradition. During this time, the Indians of this region were Munsee-speaking Lenape (Delawares), the descendants of people who had been living here for thousands of years.

Europeans identified the local bands of Indians they encountered by their geographic location referring to them as the Esopus, Haverstraws, Waoranecks, Warranawankongs, and Tappans.

The arrival of European explorers, fishermen, traders, and subsequently settlers produced dramatic cultural changes among the Indian groups in the Hudson Valley. Following contact, the Indians began to acquire European-made tools, guns, utensils, ornaments, cloth, and other items. As trade increased, they accumulated more and more European goods, and such items are frequently found on archaeological sites of this period.

The Europeans also brought diseases to which the Indians in several areas succumbed since they had no natural immunity. Wars between the Dutch and the Indians, kidnappings by Europeans, intertribal conflicts over trade, territory, and influence, and the demands for Indian lands by settlers decimated Indian populations and dispossessed many groups from their homelands. In time, these agents of instability led to a breakup of ethnic groups and the establishment of a new way of life and accommodation with the European settlers.

CHAPTER 2

NATIVE AMERICAN PRESENCE AT FORT MONTGOMERY

F ort Montgomery (1776–77), the northernmost of two Revolutionary War forts that flanked the Popolopen Creek at its confluence with the Hudson River, sat on a high bluff overlooking both. Toward the end of the Ice Age, the swift flowing water of Popolopen Creek cut a deep ravine on its journey to the Hudson creating the "twin bluffs" on which the Twin Forts were built. Near where river and creek meet are three prominent landscape features. To the east across the Hudson lies Anthony's Nose, while to the west and southwest the Popolopen Torne and Bear Mountain rise majestically above the river. The natural setting of the twin bluffs presented a commanding view of all activity on the river.

Fort Montgomery was placed on the northern bluff to prevent the British from gaining control of the Hudson Highlands during our War of Independence. American forces constructed a battery along the river; north, south, and Round Hill redoubts with connecting parapet walls; a storehouse, guardhouse, soldiers' necessary, powder magazine, bakehouse, officers' barracks, and commissary; and one- and two-story barracks. On October 6, 1777, British forces attacked the fort and after a daylong battle, captured it. Following a brief occupation, the British destroyed many of the fort's structures and then withdrew to New York City. In 1779, American forces built a small battery on top of the original battery. Aside from this, no military use was made of the site again.

Archaeological explorations at Fort Montgomery began in 1914 and continued intermittently throughout the twentieth century. Nearly all of

11

this work focused on the military history of the site, including locating and uncovering the remains of structural features. In the 1930s, Trailside staff conducted test excavations at several locations within and immediately adjacent to the fort in an effort to find evidence of Indian occupation in the area. Not surprisingly, the excavations uncovered abundant evidence of use from at least 5000 B.C. to the Historic Contact period. A chronology of the sites discovered and the artifacts found within them follows.

ROCKSHELTERS WITHIN FORT MONTGOMERY

A large boulder with a small overhang on one side sits in the eastern section of the fort on the north side of a new access road. Burggraf excavated this small shelter at some time prior to 1942. Details of this excavation are unknown but Trailside's records indicate that a projectile point and a pottery fragment were recovered from the site. These meager finds suggest limited use of this shelter during the Woodland period.

Another rockshelter is located near the edge of a flat terrace about 100 feet south-southeast of the North Redoubt. This shelter is formed by two large boulders, one leaning against the other, creating an inverted "V" with sufficient space underneath to provide protection from the elements. Jack Mead, former director of Trailside and leader of the 1967–71 excavations at the fort, reported that prehistoric artifacts were found, but the nature of these finds is not known.

RAMPARTS OF FORT MONTGOMERY

In the 1930s, Trailside staff found several prehistoric artifacts along a thirty-foot section of the Grand Battery at the fort's southwest corner. This surface collection consisted of two stemmed projectile points, one triangular point, a scraper, and several chert flakes. The location was mapped by J. H. Denniston, a park employee, and designated as Site 18-B in the Museums' inventory records.

Archaeological excavations conducted at the Grand Battery in 1971 resulted in the recovery of several projectile points and lithic debitage (waste flakes). These finds are summarized in Tables 1 and 2. They clearly indicate that Indian people intermittently occupied this area during the Middle to Terminal Archaic periods, or from around 6000 B.C. to around 1000 B.C. The recovery of two triangular Levanna-type projectile points,

TABLE 1:		STONE TOOLS RECOVERED FROM WITHIN FORT MONTGOMERY		
Location	Year	Tool/Type	Qty	Comment
Guard House	1958	projectile point/unidentified	1	broken
Main Barracks	1967	projectile point/unidentified	1	
		biface	1	
		scraper	1	
		utilized flake	1	
		hammerstone	1	
One-Story Barracks	1967	projectile point, triangular, brass	1	Historic Contact
		knife tip	1	
		utilized flakes	2	
		hammerstone	1	
		netsinker	1	
Storehouse	1968	hammerstone	1	
	2000	projectile point/unidentified	1	broken
North Redoubt	1971	projectile points/Lamoka	2	Late Archaic
		projectile point/Vosburg	1	Late Archaic
		projectile point/Genesee	1	Late Archaic
		projectile point/Stark	1	Late Archaic
		projectile point/Adena	1	Early Woodland
		projectile point/Fox Creek	1	Middle Woodland
		projectile point/Levanna	1	Late Woodland
		projectile points/unidentified	2	one-quartz
		utilized chert flake	1	
Grand Battery	1971	projectile points/Lamoka	9	Late Archaic
		projectile points/Vosburg	3	Late Archaic
		projectile points/Normanskill	2	Late Archaic
		projectile points/Bare Island	2	Late Archaic
		projectile point/Brewerton	1	Late Archaic
		projectile point/Lackawaxen (shale)	1	Late Archaic
		projectile point/Neville	1	Middle Archaic
		projectile point/Levanna	1	Late Woodland
		projectile points/unidentified	8	
		knives/bifaces	3	
		scraper	1	
		hammerstones	5	
		netsinkers	2	
	2001	projectile point, chert/Lamoka	1	Late Archaic
		projectile point, chert/ Susquehanna	1	Terminal Archaic
		scraper, chert/thumb	1	
		utilized chert flake/end	1	
Putnam's Battery	2002	utilized chert flake	1	
Service Road	2000	projectile point, chert/Madison	1	Late Woodland
Total number of projectile points			45	
Total number of knives/bifaces			5	
Total number of scrapers (formal)			3	
Total number of utilized flakes			6	
Total number of hammerstones			8	
Total number of netsinkers			3	
Grand Total			70	

one in the 1930s and the other in 1971, suggests that the site was also visited during the Late Woodland period.

In 2002, test excavations were conducted within Putnam's Battery (built in 1779), which is located to the north and adjacent to the Grand Battery. This work was performed prior to the construction of a visitors' viewing platform at this site. Chert, quartz, and jasper flakes were recovered, which indicates that tool making and repair activities took place here.

A CAMPSITE SOUTH OF THE RAMPARTS

During construction of the twin forts and the subsequent battle, a road and pontoon bridge across the creek connected Fort Clinton on the south

TABLE 2: DEBITAGE RECOVERED FROM WITHIN FORT MONTGOMERY			
Location	Year	Material	Qty
Guard House	1959	chert	2
		quartz	1
Main Barracks	1967	chert	12
One-Story Barracks	1967	chert	9
Storehouse	1968	chert	31
		jasper	1
		quartz	1
North Redoubt	1971	chert	13
		quartz	2
Powder Magazine	1968	chert	2
Grand Battery	1971	chert	3
		quartz	1
	2001	chert	63
		quartzite	4
		quartz	5
	2002	chert	58
Putnam's Battery	2002	chert	73
		quartz	5
		jasper	1
Service Road	2000	chert	5
		quartz	1
Total number of chert flakes/fragments			271
Total number of jasper flakes			2
Total number of quartz flakes			16
Total number of quartzite flakes			4
Grand Total			**293**

side of the Popolopen with Fort Montgomery on the north side. The road on the Fort Montgomery side began at the bottom of the bluff and ascended northeasterly up the steep hill until it reached a flat terrace, turned north, and entered the fort through an opening in the south parapet wall. At some time during the 1930s or 1940s, archaeological tests conducted on the flat terrace to the east of the road, below the south parapet wall, resulted in the discovery of a small prehistoric campsite. This location was mapped and entered in the Museums' records as Site 18-B-1.

The 1930s artifact collection includes the blade of a stemmed point, two scrapers, a tool blank, and one flake. All of these specimens were produced from black chert. No additional information is available on this site, but the projectile point suggests the terrace was occupied during the Late Archaic period.

On October 6, 2002, the 225th anniversary of the battle, Fort Montgomery opened to the public as an official New York State historic site. Construction of a visitor center and museum was planned near the Indian campsite. That same year, archaeologists from the New York State Office of Parks, Recreation, and Historic Preservation's (OPRHP) Bureau of Historic Sites performed test excavations in the proposed development area for additional information regarding Indian life.

These latest excavations produced important new data. Four stone tools were found, including a straight-stemmed Late Archaic-period projectile point, a chert knife, and two utilized chert flakes. These materials suggest that the Indians hunted and processed game animals here. In addition, 68 chert flakes and 13 quartz flakes were recovered, which indicates that they made or repaired tools at this location. Another important find was one fragment of Indian pottery, evidence that the site was also occupied during the Woodland period.

Artifacts recovered in 2002 were substantial and significantly added to our knowledge of this campsite. As a result, the visitor center was not built on this site, thus preserving the integrity of this prehistoric cultural resource.

A CAMPSITE NORTH OF THE FORT

The landscape on the northeast side of Fort Montgomery is steep, rugged, and covered with boulders. Here, below the bluff, is a narrow bench of land just above a small stream that flows into the Hudson. A prehistoric campsite and shell midden were discovered on this landform. It is recorded in the inventory as Site 18-B-2 and is also known as the Denniston Site.

The shell midden consisted of an accumulation of oyster shells. Indian people collected oysters in the river and brought them to this campsite where they extracted the meat and discarded the shells. Excavations here resulted in the recovery of a quartzite hammerstone and fragments of a nearly complete pottery vessel. The pot was restored and is on exhibit in the Historical Museum at Trailside (Figure 4). The pot is 5.5 inches tall, has three lugs around the rim, and has cord-marked decoration.

The small quantity of artifacts found at the site suggests that it was a seasonal, short-term, special-purpose processing camp. The shellfish meat may have been consumed on site or perhaps used as bait on hooks or in nets to attract fish in the Hudson. The pottery vessel is a type called Van Cortland Stamped and dates to the late Late Woodland period, ca. A.D. 1100 to 1700.

FIGURE 4 Restored Late Woodland pottery vessel from Fort Montgomery. Photograph by John Korbach. COURTESY PALISADES INTERSTATE PARK COMMISSION.

EXCAVATIONS AT THE FORT: 1958–2002

In 1958, Trailside staff conducted test excavations within Fort Montgomery. They investigated the Grand Battery, a small section of the powder magazine, and a guardhouse. The guardhouse was completely exposed, documented, and then reburied.

From 1967 through 1971, Jack Mead directed numerous extensive and intensive archaeological excavations at the fort. His purpose was to locate all of the Revolutionary War-era structures and features that lay buried in the area to the east of U. S. Route 9W. The primary archaeological research design was to learn as much as possible about the nature and construction of the fort's buildings and defensive ramparts so that an accurate restoration could be undertaken. Sites excavated during those years were the main barracks, powder magazine, one-story barracks, commissary, a storehouse, the North Redoubt, and the Grand Battery. All artifacts recovered from these excavations were cleaned, restored, bagged, and archived at Trailside. The planned restoration of Fort Montgomery did not take place, however, and the site returned to nature.

From 1971 to 1997, Fort Montgomery lay hidden beneath a tangle of vegetation, its historic significance and scenic views of the Hudson River lost to the public. Here in the Hudson Highlands, American forces fought a desperate battle to prevent the British from controlling the river's upper reach. Even in defeat, the fortifications and the battle to defend them served to deter reinforcement of the northern British army. Burgoyne's surrender at Saratoga, New York, thwarted British plans to seize control of the Hudson River and split the northern colonies.

In 1997, volunteers formed the Fort Montgomery Battle Site Association to promote the preservation, recognition, and interpretation of Fort Montgomery. This organization, in conjunction with the Palisades Interstate Park Commission and OPRHP, worked to stabilize the excavated ruins and open the area for public visitation. Their efforts included clearing dead trees and brush, constructing an access road, trails, and footbridge over the Popolopen, and installing viewpoints with interpretive signs. Archaeological investigations were conducted within all areas prior to the start of any construction activity.

Excavations at Fort Montgomery from 1958 to 2002 focused on the delineation of historic period cultural features and the recovery of related artifacts. No Native American cultural features such as hearths have been found, but numerous artifacts of Indian origin were recovered (Figure

FIGURE 5 Projectile points and stone sinker (bottom) found at the Grand Battery and North Redoubt during the 1967–1971 excavations at Fort Montgomery. COURTESY NEW YORK STATE OFFICE OF PARKS, RECREATION AND HISTORIC PRESERVATION.

5). Locations and descriptions of these artifacts are presented in Tables 1 and 2.

A total of 45 projectile points and point fragments were recovered from the Revolutionary War structures and features that were investigated. Many of these points are recognized types that have been documented and dated elsewhere: Neville, Stark, Lamoka, Vosburg, Genesee, Normanskill, Bare Island, Brewerton, Lackawaxen, Susquehanna, Adena, Fox Creek, Levanna, and Madison. One triangular-shaped brass projectile point recovered from the site of the one-story barracks indicates continued use of Indian technology with a new material produced in Europe. The range of point types reveals occupation by Indians often and intermittently from around 5000 B.C. to around A.D. 1750.

In addition to projectile points, other chipped-stone tools recovered include bifaces and knives, formal scrapers, and utilized flakes that were informal expedient items also used as scrapers or knives. Eight hammerstones and three stone sinkers were also recovered.

The site produced a considerable quantity of lithic debitage. The primary lithic material used for making stone tools was chert in various shades of black and gray. Small quantities of quartz, quartzite, jasper, and shale were unearthed, suggesting that these materials were used as well.

Lithic raw materials found consisted of quarried chert (primary) brought in from elsewhere and cobble chert (secondary or glacially deposited) that could have been obtained locally. Debitage found includes fragments and shatter, primary and secondary cortical fragments and flakes, tertiary flakes, and small thinning flakes. Analysis of these types indicates that all stages of tool manufacturing or maintenance and repair took place here.

Artifacts recovered from the various excavations within Fort Montgomery provide abundant evidence that Indian people periodically occupied the area from the Middle Archaic period into the Historic Contact period. They were here long before the arrival of the Europeans, and before the site was developed as a fort in 1776.

The distribution of recovered artifacts reveals that several locations were utilized as campsites, including flat terraces on the north and south sides of the fort, two rockshelters within the fort proper, and other flat well-drained areas. Most of the stone tool and waste flakes came from the Grand Battery and Putnam's Battery, which suggests that this was a primary location for a camp overlooking the river.

Prehistoric occupants of the fort site most likely procured potable water from a mountain stream that flows down to the Hudson just to the north of the fort. Another freshwater source may have been a natural spring located at the fort's western edge. This spring, later identified as a "spring head" on Revolutionary War-era maps, was a source of drinking water for the Historic period occupants of Fort Montgomery.

Functional analysis of the tools indicates that the acquisition of subsistence resources and their processing occurred at the site. The presence of projectile points and stone sinkers suggests that small groups of travelers engaged in hunting and fishing on a short-term basis. The lack of cultural features such as hearths, post molds, and storage or refuse pits, together with a paucity of pottery (only one fragment has been found), supports the conclusion that the occupations here were brief.

CHAPTER 3

INDIAN CAMPSITES
AT FORT CLINTON

The Appalachian Trail passes over Bear Mountain, through Trailside, across the Bear Mountain Bridge, and over Anthony's Nose. The trail, museum exhibits, and paths offer hikers, day-trippers, and casual visitors an opportunity to study the natural environment and rich history of the area. Everyone literally walks through a long era of human history.

Indian peoples were the first to camp on the scenic bluff above the river, later the site of Fort Clinton during the Revolutionary War. After the war, Eugene Lucet built a dwelling amid the ruins of Fort Clinton. By 1834, the Pell family occupied this country estate and erased most of the fort's physical remains. In 1889, a railroad bridge spanning the Hudson was proposed across the Pell property and fort site. Construction of the bridge was started but quickly halted due to financial difficulties. The Pell Mansion, as it became known, burned in 1910, by which time it had sunk to the lowly status of a boarding house. In 1923–24, the Bear Mountain Bridge was constructed and, together with an approach road from the west (now Route 6), cut through the heart of the fort, the battle-field, and the Pell estate.

In 1927, the bluff near the bridge was chosen as the location for Trailside Museums, the Bear Mountain Zoo, and nature trails. By 1950, the present complex of stone buildings, winding paths, animal enclosures, and overlooks had been constructed.

During this extensive and intensive period of activity, several Indian campsites were discovered along the bluff and within the site of Fort Clinton and its battlefield.

EXCAVATIONS AT THE OUTER (WEST) REDOUBT

Archaeological excavations at the Outer Redoubt began in 1935. The purpose of these excavations was to delineate this Revolutionary War-period earthwork so that it could be restored and interpreted to the public. William H. Carr, director of Trailside; Richard J. Koke, historian; James D. Burggraf, archaeologist; Jesse H. Denniston, William Ossman, and others conducted these excavations (Figure 6). Work continued intermittently until 1939, by which time all of the major features of the redoubt were uncovered, stabilized, and reconstructed. During the excavations, numerous artifacts were recovered including cannon and musket balls, grapeshot, gun parts, gun flints, lead strips, buttons, nails, clay tobacco pipe fragments, bottle fragments, bone fragments, and Indian stone tools and flakes.

The Indian artifacts found at the Outer Redoubt included 12 complete and fragmentary projectile points, six stone scrapers, two knife blades, three tool blanks, and a fragment of pottery. In their report, Koke and Burggraf noted that the raw materials used by the Indians to make stone tools were black chert, gray chert, slate, and yellow jasper. The projectile-point types

FIGURE 6 James D. Burggraf and Jesse H. Denniston excavating in the Outer Redoubt of Fort Clinton in 1936. COURTESY PALISADES INTERSTATE PARK COMMISSION.

found at the site, described as "arrowheads" by the excavators, were Brewerton-Eared Triangle and Triangular, or Levanna. They wrote, "Most of the finds came from sections of the redoubt whose floor level had been constructed from earth evidently secured from the pockets in the immediate vicinity of the defense." A few specimens were also found in undisturbed rock crevices not affected by the construction of the Outer Redoubt.

Projectile points recovered from the site, together with the one fragment of pottery, indicate two periods of occupation by Indian peoples: the Late Archaic period of prehistoric cultural history (ca. 4000–1000 B.C.) and during the Late Woodland period (ca. A.D. 1000–1600). The projectile points suggest that hunting was a major activity of the people who camped here. The presence of flakes indicates that stone tools were made or refurbished here. Six stone scrapers (formal tools) were found at the site. Indians used them to work raw materials such as wood, bone, and hides.

THE HISTORICAL MUSEUM

The Historical Museum was constructed in 1934 on the site of the nineteenth-century Pell House and within the Star Redoubt of Fort Clinton on the bluff overlooking the Hudson River. During construction, Museums' staff recovered "an Indian scraper, a drill, a broken arrowpoint and a few chips [i.e., flakes]."

In 1992, 33 shovel test units were excavated along the fence on the north side of the Historical Museum between the service entrance gate and the edge of the bluff. Indian artifacts were recovered from four test units along the fence north-northeast of the museum. The finds included two utilized chert flakes which were used as scrapers, one gray chert thumb scraper, and one utilized gray chert flake that functioned as a knife. Other lithic materials recovered included a gray chert core, gray and black chert fragments, and black and gray primary, tertiary, and retouch flakes. Analysis of the tools and waste flakes showed that all stages of tool making from local materials took place here.

THE MINI-BUS/ADA PARKING AREA SITE

In 1992, 39 shovel test units were excavated immediately to the north of the Geology Museum. The objectives of this investigation were to locate and identify any cultural resources that might be present within the area, to evaluate their research potential and significance, and to evaluate the effects of the proposed construction of an ADA (Americans with Disabilities Act) parking area on the cultural resources.

Specimens of prehistoric origin found within the area include a granite abrader, a pebble hammerstone, a quartzite hammerstone, a gray-black basalt flake, a gray chert fragment, a utilized gray chert flake that functioned as a side scraper, and one grayish-brown chert flake. No prehistoric cultural features or diagnostic artifacts were found, however, the presence of a few tools and a chert flake and fragment suggests that this site might have been a workshop. All of the prehistoric artifacts were found in mixed cultural and disturbed physical contexts. As a result, the ADA parking area was constructed as planned.

THE FORT CLINTON PREHISTORIC SITE

In 1992, as part of a program of service access improvements at the Bear Mountain Bridge and Trailside, test excavations were conducted in the area planned for parking spaces. Fifty-eight shovel test pits and fourteen 5' x 5' test units were dug prior to the start of construction, resulting in the recovery of numerous prehistoric and historic artifacts. The tests revealed two discrete cultural components: a historic site within the center of the proposed parking lot and a prehistoric site to the west.

Three outcrops of bedrock in a flat wooded area—one to the northwest and two on the south—surrounded the prehistoric component. This site was designated the Fort Clinton Prehistoric Site. Sixteen shovel test pits and eight test units revealed that the site measured 40' x 30', or 1,200 square feet.

A total of 401 artifacts of Native American origin were recovered. This prehistoric assemblage is divided for analytical convenience into a number of classes such as projectile points, bifaces, flake tools, cores, cobble tools, debitage, and ceramics. Forty-four prehistoric stone tools were recovered and are described in Table 3.

PROJECTILE POINTS

One complete projectile point, one point with its tip broken off and missing, one reworked point, and three projectile-point fragments were recovered and analyzed (Table 3). Three projectile points are recognized types that have been documented and date to the Late to Terminal

Archaic periods. These types include two Poplar Island points and a broken Snook Kill point. The Poplar Island points were made from argillite, and the Snook Kill point from dark gray chert.

BIFACES

This class of artifacts represents pieces of stone that have been flaked on both sides and whose specific function cannot be ascertained. Three complete bifaces were recovered from the site: one was oval-shaped and made from granite, one was a preform made of gray-brown chert, and one was a preform made of red shale. One large blank, made from gray-brown chert, was also found and shows evidence of wear along one edge, but its function could not be determined.

Four biface fragments were found. One, made of gray-brown chert, may be a broken drill, while another, made of dark gray chert, appeared to be the round end of a large blade. A third biface fragment of gray argillite was possibly the midsection of a large blade. Finally, a tip and blade fragment of tan chert may be part of a formal tool, possibly a projectile point or knife.

KNIFE

A flake knife was found in Test Unit 6, Stratum II. This tool, manufactured from gray chert, measures 53 mm x 37 mm x 13 mm. It has a curved cutting edge and use wear was evident in the form of edge crushing.

FORMAL SCRAPERS

Eight scrapers were found at the site (Figure 7). Scrapers are tools that were unifacially flaked specifically to be pulled or dragged across the material being worked at right angles to the cutting edge. These scrapers were deliberately manufactured in a purposeful manner and are characterized by low, nearly uniform unifacial retouch on a segment of a flake or fragment.

One specimen was an end scraper made from green Normanskill chert. Another end scraper had an excurvate edge and was made of gray chert. These tools show finely retouched edges.

Five small thumb scrapers were found, three made from black chert, one from gray-black chert, and one from tan chert. Three of the thumb scrapers have steep work edges, while the other two have low edge angles.

Tool	Type	Material and Color	Dimensions (mm) L.W.T.	Comments
Abrader		granite, gray	62 x 30 x 14	polished edge
Abrader (?)		shale, gray	34 x 28 x 7	two grooves
Biface	oval shape	granite, gray	50 x 26 x 11	function unknown
Biface	preform	chert, gray/brown	57 x 36 x 14	
Biface	preform	shale, red	54 x 33 x 7	
Biface fragment	possible drill	chert, gray/brown	32 x 13 x 6	broken
Core	cobble	quartzite, gray	61 x 43 x 31	cortex present
Core	pebble	chert, gray	44 x 28 x 16	cortex present, two pieces conjoined
Hammerstone	cobble	quartzite, gray	64 x 50 x 30	broken
Hammerstone	cobble	quartzite, tan	80 x 60 x 51	broken
Hammerstone	cobble	quartzite, gray/brown	70 x 66 x 42	
Knife	flake	chert, gray	53 x 37 x 13	
Projectile point fragment	tip	chert, black	23 x 16 x 5	broken
Scraper	end	chert, green	45 x 45 x 8	Normanskill chert
Scraper	thumb	chert, black	31 x 26 x 8	
Utilized flake	scraper	chert, black	24 x 18 x 4	
Utilized flake	scraper	chert, black	24 x 22 x 11	
Utilized flake	scraper	chert, gray	24 x 23 x 6	
Utilized flake	scraper	chert, gray	61 x 44 x 13	
Utilized flake	scraper	chert, gray/black	34 x 26 x 13	
Utilized flake	abrader(?)	shale, gray/brown	112 x 37 x 7	two pieces conjoined

TABLE 3 CONTINUED

Tool	Type	Material and Color	Dimensions (mm) L.W.T.	Comments
Core	biface	chert, gray/black	45 x 43 x 17	striking platform
Biface fragment	blade tip (?)	chert, dark gray	31 x 42 x 7	broken
Hammerstone	cobble	sandstone, brown	120 x 76 x 47	cortex present
Core	cobble	chert, brown	37 x 29 x 22	
Scraper	end	chert, gray	36 x 31 x 7	
Projectile point	Poplar Island	argillite, gray	47 x 22 x 7	tip missing; Terminal Archaic
Projectile point	Poplar Island	argillite, gray	46 x 24 x 8	Terminal Archaic
Scraper	thumb	chert, black	28 x 24 x 10	steep edge
Scraper	thumb	chert, black	25 x 20 x 10	steep edge
Scraper	thumb	chert, gray/black	31 x 26.5 x 7	steep edge
Scraper	thumb	chert, tan	25 x 23 x 6	
Projectile point/drill	retouched	chert, black	28 x 16.5 x 5	untyped
Utilized flake	scraper	chert, black	36 x 25 x 7	
Utilized flake	scraper	chert, gray/brown	41 x 36 x 13	
Utilized flake	scraper	chert, black	38 x 11 x 5	
Scraper	side	chert, green/brown	34 x 28 x 8	Normanskill chert
Projectile point fragment	Snook Kill	chert, dark gray	26 x 27 x 6	Late Archaic
Projectile point fragment	triang. blade	chert, black	36 x 28 x 8	broken
Biface fragment	tip and blade	shale, tan	58 x 25 x 5	
Utilized flake		chert, gray	14 x 11 x 3	function unknown
Utilized flake		argillite, gray	64 x 37 x 10	linear scars
Blank		chert, gray/brown	40 x 38 x 10	edge wear present
Biface fragment		argillite, gray	37 x 30 x 6	

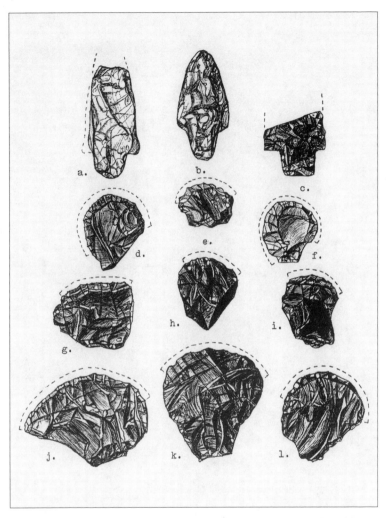

FIGURE 7 Projectile points, knife, and formal scrapers from the Fort Clinton Prehistoric Site: (a–b) Poplar Island projectile points, gray argillite; (c) Snook Kill projectile-point base, dark gray chert; (d) thumb scraper, gray-black chert; (e) steep edge thumb scraper, black chert; (f) thumb scraper, gray-black chert; (g) side scraper, green-brown chert; (h) thumb scraper, black chert; (i) steep edge thumb scraper, black chert; (j) knife, gray chert; (k) end scraper, green Norman-skill chert; (l) end scraper, gray chert. Dotted line (- - -) indicates area of use wear. Drawing by Tom Fitzpatrick. Illustration reduced from original.

One side scraper was recovered. It was fashioned from a dark brown-green chert, possibly Normanskill, and measures 34 mm x 28 mm x 8 mm. This tool is generally rectangular in plan and wedge-shaped in cross-section, with a finely retouched side edge. It was difficult to detect use wear on this tool, but the working edge appeared to have slight scarring and polish.

UTILIZED FLAKES

There are 11 utilized flakes in the Fort Clinton collection. They are irregularly shaped with varying degrees of edge wear. Only one distinctive tool class was recognized within this collection: scrapers. Eight specimens are scrapers whose function was determined on the basis of visible use-wear patterns. One utilized flake tool consists of two conjoining pieces of gray shale, measuring 112 mm x 37 mm x 7 mm, with some polish and striations on one flat side, suggesting it may have been used as an abrader.

The function of two utilized flakes could not be determined. One is a small gray chert flake with slight evidence of use wear. The other is a gray argillite flake measuring 64 mm x 37 mm x 10 mm with one linear scar on each flat surface.

As noted earlier, the shapes of these tools are irregular and are by-products from the manufacture of chipped-stone tools. These flakes were probably picked up and selected for use primarily because of their edge sharpness. They were not used for very long, nor were they resharpened. They were simply expedient tools and were quickly discarded.

HAMMERSTONES

Four hammerstones were recovered from Fort Clinton. Specimen number one was a broken gray quartzite cobble that measures 64 mm x 50 mm x 30 mm, with battering evident on the broken surface. Number two was also a broken quartzite cobble and measures 80 mm x 60 mm x 51 mm, with battering in evidence at one end. A complete quartzite hammerstone was also found, measuring 70 mm x 66 mm x 42 mm. The extensive battering and wear at one end indicates prolonged use. A brown sandstone hammerstone that measures 120 mm x 76 mm x 47 mm was extensively battered at one end and had a piece broken off on the opposite end. All of these hammerstones were clearly used as percussion tools.

CORES

Four cores were recovered and are described in Table 3. Two are cobble cores, one is a pebble core, and one is a biface core with a clear striking platform. The cobble and pebble cores have cortex present on their exterior surface.

ABRADERS

Two abraders were recovered. One of gray-colored granite measures 62 mm x 30 mm x 14 mm. Use wear in the form of a polished surface was evident along one lateral edge. The second specimen was somewhat problematical. It is a piece of gray shale, 34 mm x 28 mm x 7 mm with two parallel grooves on one flat surface. No striations within the grooves were discerned under low-power magnification.

DEBITAGE

Lithic debitage, the discarded by-product of stone-tool manufacturing and refurbishing, was found in every excavation unit and in nearly every stratum. Analysis of the lithic assemblage included sorting, measuring, and counting the specimens. All lithic identification was done at the hand specimen level by visual inspection. Identifications are purely descriptive. The purpose of this was to determine the types of raw materials used by the site's occupants, to trace the distribution of debitage across the site, and to determine the stage or stages of tool manufacture or refurbishing.

A total of 1,357 flakes and fragments were recovered during the excavations. Black and gray colored cherts were clearly the dominant lithic types accounting for 83.1% of the total debitage recovered. Black chert was the predominant choice (34.64%), followed by gray-brown chert (22.55%), dark gray chert (16.58%), gray chert (6.56%), and gray-black chert (2.73%). Table 4 presents an analysis of the raw materials utilized at the site.

In addition to identifying raw materials, the debitage was sorted by type, namely fragments or shatter, fragments with cortex, primary and

Material	Quantity	% of Total
Black Chert	470	34.64
Gray-Brown Chert	306	22.55
Dark Gray Chert	225	16.58
Gray Chert	89	6.56
Quartz	86	6.34
Gray-Black Chert	37	2.73
Gray-Brown-Tan Shale	36	2.65
Green Chert	26	1.92
Red Shale	25	1.84
Brown Chert	19	1.40
Tan Chert	18	1.33
Red Jasper	11	0.81
Quartzite	5	0.37
Granite-Gneiss	3	0.22
Argillite	1	0.07
Totals	**1,357**	**100.00**

secondary cortical flakes, tertiary flakes, and retouch or thinning flakes. These six types of debitage correlate well with prehistoric knapping operations or quarrying of the raw material, edging, decortication, thinning, and resharpening or retouching.

The data in Table 5 shows the types and frequency of flakes and fragments recovered. One hundred forty-seven specimens in the collection are cortical flakes and fragments that were struck from pebbles and cobbles. These specimens comprise 10.84% of the total debitage found. In addition, Table 5 clearly shows that all stages of tool manufacturing occurred there.

The analysis of debitage by size supports the conclusion that all stages of tool manufacturing took place at the site.

The data in Table 6 indicate that the majority of flakes in the collection were small—that is, less than 30 mm in maximum length. These specimens account for nearly 85 percent of the total debitage collection.

Debitage was found in nearly all shovel tests and in all test units, however, the density of these artifacts varies from unit to unit. The most

TABLE 5:	ANALYSIS OF DEBITAGE BY TYPE RECOVERED FROM THE FORT CLINTON PREHISTORIC SITE	
Type	Quantity	% of Total
Fragments/Shatter	327	24.10
Fragments with Cortex	51	3.76
Primary Cortical Flakes	64	4.72
Secondary Cortical Flakes	32	2.36
Tertiary Flakes	664	48.93
Retouch/Thinning Flakes	219	16.14
Totals	1,357	100.00

TABLE 6:	ANALYSIS OF DEBITAGE BY SIZE RECOVERED FROM THE FORT CLINTON PREHISTORIC SITE	
Size	Quantity	% of Total
Less than 10 mm	32	2.36
10 – less than 30 mm	1,114	82.10
30 – 60 mm	206	15.18
More than 60 mm	5	0.37
Totals	1,357	100.00

significant concentration of debitage was in Test Unit 10, where 345 specimens were found. There was also a high concentration of flakes in Test Unit 12.

CERAMIC FRAGMENT

One fragment of prehistoric pottery was recovered. The sherd is very small and quartz tempered, and has a fine dentate stamped decoration.

TRADE BEAD

One glass trade bead was recovered from Test Unit 1, Stratum I, within the eighteenth-century historic deposit to the east of the prehistoric site. This specimen is ruby red in color, measures 5 mm in diameter, and is classified as type IIa5, according to a system developed by Kenneth and Martha Ann Kidd.

ANALYSIS AND INTERPRETATION

The Fort Clinton Prehistoric Site yielded three diagnostic projectile points indicating that it was occupied intermittently in the Late and Terminal Archaic periods (ca. 3000–1000 B.C.). The dentate-stamped pottery fragment and glass trade bead suggest that the site was visited and used during the Late Woodland and Historic Contact periods (ca. A.D. 1000–1750).

Prehistoric Fort Clinton had several topographic and environmental features that were highly desirable factors in the Indians' site selection process. The land was elevated and flat, and the soil was well drained. It was situated about 560 feet west of the Hudson River. Popolopen Creek, a freshwater stream, flowed into the Hudson just north of the site, and Hessian Lake was to the southwest. Thus, fresh water was readily available, and the adjacent woodlands, river, stream, and lake would have provided the Indians with a large variety of flora and fauna for use as food and raw materials.

The soils in the area are very stony. Glacially derived pebbles and cobbles, particularly those of chert and quartz, provided an abundant supply of raw material for tool making. Prehistoric toolmakers undoubtedly procured their raw materials from the surface, the surrounding area, and the shores of the Popolopen and the Hudson. The presence of 147 cortical flakes and fragments indicates that they utilized pebble and cobble raw materials to manufacture tools. This was a patterned adaptation to the Highlands where crystalline and metamorphic materials in cobble form occur abundantly and can be acquired with a brief expenditure of energy.

Non-local lithic materials such as green Normanskill chert, red jasper, and argillite were present in very small quantities. The presence of these materials may reflect glacial or human transport or trade.

The analysis of stone tools and debitage clearly shows that all stages of tool manufacturing took place at the site. We infer that the cobble reduction sequence in the manufacture of tools included the following operations:

1. **PROCUREMENT:** The prehistoric knapper found cobbles of chert on the surface;
2. **COBBLE DECORTICATION:** The knapper struck the chert cobbles with a hammerstone, producing primary and secondary flakes from the core and blocky fragments or shatter;

3. THINNING: Large flakes and fragments were bifacially reduced by percussion to form tool blanks and preforms;
4. FINAL SHAPING: Further reduction was obtained by trimming and thinning biface edges with a pressure-flaking technique.

The debitage evidence argues heavily for late-stage lithic reduction processes or reworking activities. The primary lithic technology included tool completion and reworking. Although cores, blanks, and preforms were found and produced at the site, some were most likely brought in as part of previously made tool kits. These blanks or preforms were then converted into completed tools. Also, completed tools were probably brought to the site and may have been refurbished or reworked when they were no longer usable due to breakage, dulling, or other use damage. One such reworked tool is present in the Fort Clinton Prehistoric Site collection.

A functional analysis of the recovered tools was undertaken to gain insight into subsistence-related activities at the site. The use of projectile points as actual hunting implements is assumed. However, one specimen, a Snook Kill-type point, was broken transversely across the blade, which suggests that it may have been used as a prying tool.

Eight formal scrapers were found. The large end scraper made of green Normanskill chert has an excurvate low-angle working edge with moderate use wear, which suggests that it was drawn over soft surfaces with moderate pressure. This tool may have been hafted. A second end scraper of gray chert also has an excurvate working edge but with a steep angle. This specimen shows moderate use wear and was hand-held as it was drawn over a soft surface. A side scraper of dark brown-green chert is wedge-shaped, has a low edge angle, and shows minimal use wear. It, too, was probably hand-held. The five small thumb scrapers have steep edge angles; they were probably hand-held and may have been used on tough or resistant material such as wood, antler, or bone.

The largest functional category of tools from the site is that of utilized flakes. All of these irregularly shaped tools have low edge angles and were used as scrapers on both hard and soft material. They were lightly and briefly used and then discarded.

Four hammerstones, which are percussion tools, were found at the site. Evidence of battering is present on each cobble, and all appear to be the type associated with working stone.

A large flake knife made of gray chert shows much evidence of use wear in the form of edge crushing and polish of both sides of the cutting blade near its edge. This tool was probably hand-held.

In summary, the functional range of these tools is very limited. No hearths or other habitation features were found; no evidence suggests that food processing or consumption took place here. The hammerstones are clearly related to tool manufacturing itself. The scrapers, utilized flakes, and knife may be related to the production of subsistence-related equipment such as wooden shafts, handles, or bone implements. We conclude that individuals or small bands of hunters and gatherers used the site as a tool production area. Their principal activity was procuring and reducing locally available lithic resources, primarily chert cobbles, into tools.

The stratigraphic and typological evidence (three diagnostic points, one fragment of pottery, and a trade bead) indicates several short-term occupations at this site, which is small and extremely shallow. The diagnostic artifacts are evidence of successional use of the area during the Late and Terminal Archaic periods and the Late Woodland and Historic Contact periods. This tool workshop was part of a network of temporarily occupied sites within an overall pattern of sites related to the hunting-and-gathering subsistence economy practiced in this region throughout all cultural-historic periods.

CAMPSITES ALONG THE BLUFF

During the Late Archaic and Late Woodland cultural periods, Indian peoples camped along a section of the bluff located east of the Bear Den. This site is flat to gently sloping and overlooks the Hudson River (Figure 8). Stone tools, including projectile points, bifaces, pebble hammerstones, and knives, have been recovered from this area and are displayed in a nearby exhibit. Traces of Indian occupation have also been found along the edge of the bluff near the entrance to Trailside. Artifacts found were chert flakes, the residue of tool making or refurbishing.

HESSIAN LAKE

Hessian Lake is located about 1,000 feet west of the Hudson River and about 350 feet above it. A natural body of water, it is one-half mile long, about 700 feet wide, and about 35 feet deep. On eighteenth- and nineteenth-century maps, the lake is identified as a "Pond," "Bear Hill Pond," and "Highland Lake."

In 1846, the Orange County historian Samuel Eager noted that the lake was once known by its Indian name "Sinnipink." In 1872, the historian E. M. Ruttenber described the lake as "a small rivulet called by ye Indians Assinnapink," which was said to mean "the stream from the solid rocks." More recently, the Lenape scholar and linguist Raymond Whritenour, proprietor of Lenape Texts and Studies in Butler, New Jersey, stated that "Assinnapink" is a Munsee word that means "the place of the stony water." As Hessian Lake is located along the eastern base of Bear Mountain and has a sheer vertical ledge on its west side, both interpretations appear to describe it accurately.

An island was once situated just off the northeastern shore of Hessian Lake. Its size, shape, and offshore location are shown on the 1914 development map of Bear Mountain State Park. In 1936, the archaeologist Max Schrabisch stated, "there are traces of a campsite at the northern end of Hessian Lake." This island no longer exists, as the area between it and the shore has been filled in. Today, it is a rock outcrop that is used by picnickers and anglers.

FIGURE 8 An Indian campsite on the bluff at Trailside. Photograph by Edward J. Lenik (2002).

On September 13, 1993, a scuba diver recovered a hand-carved wooden bowl from about 18 inches of silty mud at the bottom of Hessian Lake. She found the bowl about 100 feet from the north end of the lake, near the east shore, at a water depth of approximately 30 feet. Carved from a maple log, probably one-half of a split log, the bowl is rectangular with slightly rounded ends (Figure 9). The ends and sides taper down to a flat bottom on the exterior. The bowl measures 14.5 inches in length, 7 inches in width, and 3 inches in height. Its interior is hollowed out to form a trough 9.5 inches in length at the top, tapering to 7 inches at the bottom. It has a maximum interior depth of 2 inches and a volume of about one quart.

The bowl was carved with metal tools. The exterior was cut with a sharp ax; the interior appears to have been shaped with a crooked metal knife, adze, or curved chisel. Portions of the exterior and interior are black as the result of charring. No attempt was made by the carver to smooth or finish the bowl. It lacks overall symmetry and is primitive in appearance.

The bowl was likely a vessel for campsite use, made from necessity, probably in close proximity to the lake—perhaps on the island campsite at the north end. Its function was in food preparation and/or consumption, and probably held a liquid such as stew.

Analysis of the log bowl by a professional woodcarver and this author leads to the deduction that it is of Indian origin because of its primitive form and method of manufacture. It probably dates to the Historic Contact period, or from about A.D. 1600–1700. An ethnohistoric account of Indian lifeways in New York lends weight to these conclusions. A 1644 Dutch account of the Mohawk Indians states, "When they travel they take with them their maize (corn), a kettle, a wooden bowl and a spoon; these they pack up and hang on their backs." A late seventeenth-century description of Indians making woodenware notes that "when the savages are about to make Wooden Dishes, Porringers or Spoons, they form the Wood to their Purpose with their stone hatchets, make it hollow with their Coles out of the Fire and scrape them afterward with Beaver's Teeth for to polish them." This was the manufacturing process used to produce the log bowl found in Hessian Lake but metal tools were used instead of stone and animal teeth. The exterior of the bowl is blackened, suggesting that it was burned after it was shaped.

POPOLOPEN CREEK

In 1872, Ruttenber called Popolopen Creek "Pooploop's kil" and suggested it was the name of an Indian owner. Whritenour recently speculated that the creek's name might be derived from the Munsee word "pehpaalapuw," meaning "it overflows continually." During the Historic Contact period, the inhabitants of this region were Munsee-speaking Lenape or Delawares, descendants of Indian people who had been living here for thousands of years.

Popolopen Creek begins at Stillwell Lake, within the West Point Military Reservation, and flows southeast, then south, until it reaches the site of the historic Queensboro Furnace. It then turns and flows east through a gorge and empties into the Hudson River. Before Euro-American settlement in the region, the creek was a gateway to the interior for Indian peoples.

In the 1930s, two prehistoric campsites were discovered on the south side of Popolopen Creek about 500 feet west of where the creek joins the river. Excavated by Burggraf, Denniston, and others in 1935 and 1937, both were situated on small, flat terraces, one about 5 feet above the level of the creek, and the other about 15 feet above the water.

Twenty-six complete projectile points and two broken tips were recovered from these sites. The identified diagnostic point types in the

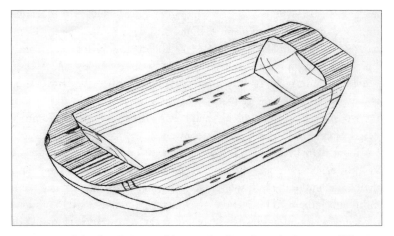

FIGURE 9 A log bowl recovered by a scuba diver from the bottom of Hessian Lake in Bear Mountain State Park. Views: top, inside; middle side; bottom. Drawing by Tom Fitzpatrick.

site collection include Brewerton side-notched, Bare Island, Normanskill, Lamoka, and Vosburg, all of which date to the Late Archaic period. Also recovered was one Orient Fishtail point, which dates to the Terminal Archaic to Early Woodland periods, and three triangular points that date to the Late Woodland period.

Other stone tools were found including a drill tip, 15 scrapers, and a small thumbnail scraper. Twenty-one pieces of debitage were also recovered. The site collection contains 19 pottery fragments containing incised decorations. The pot sherds date to the Late Woodland period.

Analysis of the artifact collection indicates that the Popolopen Creek outlet sites were short-term, multi-component, limited-function sites. They were occupied by small groups of Late Archaic and Woodland period hunters as temporary travel camps or as campsites for procuring various nearby resources. From these strategic locations near the Hudson River, individual hunting-and-gathering parties could forage in the surrounding area for food and other materials.

A limited range of artifacts was recovered, which suggests that activities were also limited and focused on small-scale procurement and processing of subsistence resources. The presence of projectile points indicates that fauna was hunted nearby. Tools were also made or repaired here. These two campsites were selected because the land was low-lying, flat, well drained, easily accessible by water, and adjacent to the food resources of the creek and river.

One can easily visualize a canoe on the Hudson River approaching the mouth of the Popolopen Creek in pre-Columbian times: Indians paddling swiftly and tirelessly, propelling their craft forward toward the outlet of the creek. A hawk soars overhead in the bright sunlight. Turning, the canoe enters the creek, and the Indians see a dark, shadowy, mysterious forest on the steep bluffs of each bank. In the shadows of the trees they spot deer at the water's edge. They beach the canoe on the south bank and exclaim, "This is a good place to camp."

CAMPSITES BELOW THE BLUFF

The topography of the Trailside Museums area overlooking the Hudson River consists of steep, high bluffs. Local elevations along the bluff range from 120 feet to 180 feet above river level, which is at mean sea level. The ground surface consists of exposed granitic bedrock and shallow soils.

Several swales extend down the steep slopes toward the river, which is tidal. The slopes range from 35 to 60 degrees and contain numerous rocks and boulders of variable size.

By the middle of the nineteenth century, an ice industry flourished in the area. Blocks of ice cut from Hessian Lake were transported down the slope to an icehouse for eventual shipment by boat to New York City. In 1910, the Park Commission built a dock to accommodate excursion boats coming to the new Bear Mountain Park. In 1911, the West Shore Railroad built the Bear Mountain Railroad Station near the dock.

Two rockshelters, discovered at the bottom of the bluff and excavated by Burggraf, were named after this station.

THE "POT" SHELTER

During World War II, Burggraf worked for the New York Central Railroad as part of a crew that was rebuilding trestles to the north and south of Iona Island. In 1944, Burggraf discovered this rockshelter while observing the "toilet" activities of a track-laying gang. Many years later, he described his find in the Trailside Museums Historical Papers (#H-15.90). Here is Burggraf's report in his own words:

> One night after work, I walked the mile from camp and found their impromptu latrine. There was a recess of some 10 feet by 12 feet running back from the railroad, and surrounded on three sides by the sheer rock face. To make it interesting, the overhang formed a fair rockshelter.
>
> At the first opportunity, I revisited the spot and carefully removed the recent traces of modern man. Then, . . . I removed the overburden of coal cinders from a 5 foot square section against the rear wall of the shelter. Almost at once I saw some sherds of a broken Indian pot. Then trowelling, I recovered several more fragments of the same vessel. As these were fragments from both the rim and base, it was evident the pot had been damaged beyond any hope of future use to its makers.
>
> There was no evidence that the shelter was occupied for more than a day or two as there was no refuse or the usual profusion of waste flakes resulting from projectile point manufacture.

Every foot of the floor area was carefully trowelled and then sifted, until the edge of the ballasted railroad bed prevented . . . digging.

Burggraf speculated that a small party of Indians, traveling by canoe on the river, sought shelter here during a storm and accidentally broke their cooking vessel. He noted that the pot was too large and too fragile to be carried through the forest. Thus, it must have been carried by canoe, which was the only way to gain access to the rockshelter.

A sufficient quantity of sherds was recovered from this site to permit restoration of the pot. It is conical, measuring 11 inches in height and 13 inches in diameter across the top (Figure 10). The interior and exterior surfaces are cord wrapped paddle marked. A large vertical crack is present on one side, which was repaired by drilling a hole on each side and lacing the break together. The vessel is a type called Vinette I that dates to the Early Woodland period (ca. 1000 B.C.–A.D. 1).

The restored vessel is on exhibit in the Historical Museum at Trailside. The rockshelter is designated Site 10-B in the Museum's inventory.

FIGURE 10 Restored conical pot from the Bear Mountain Railroad Station Rockshelter. COURTESY PALISADES INTERSTATE PARK COMMISSION.

This small rockshelter is located to the south of the "Pot" Shelter and is situated about 30 feet above the railroad tracks. Archaeological excavations here resulted in the recovery of three Fox Creek Stemmed-type and one Fox Creek Lanceolate-type projectile points, a broken knife, and two pieces of debitage.

The scarcity of cultural material suggests it was occupied very briefly by a few individuals. Based on the type of projectile points found, we infer that the site was visited during the Middle Woodland period (ca. A.D. 1–1000).

CHAPTER 4

WANAKAWAGHKIN
(IONA ISLAND)

On July 13, 1683, Sakaghkewerk, Sachem of Haverstraw, together with other Indians, sold a large tract of land "on the west side of Hudson River within the Highlands over against Anthony's Nose" for the sum of "six shillings current silver money" and for "divers other valuable causes and considerations" to Stephanus Van Cortlandt, a merchant in the City of New York. Indian witnesses and signatories to the sale, in addition to the sachem, were Werekepes, Sagnoghharmp, Kakeras, Kaghtsikoos, and Mantion.

The deed of sale described this tract as "beginning on the south side of a creek called Senkapogh and soe alongst the said creek to the head thereof and then northerly along the high hills . . . to another creek called Assinipink [Hessian Lake] and from thence along the said creek to the Hudson River again, together with a certain Island and parcel of meadow land near or adjoining to the same called Wanakawaghkin and by the Christians known by the name of Salisbury's Island." Whritenour states that the name Senkapogh means "angle rock" or "cornered rock." This tract of land is now Bear Mountain State Park, and Salisbury's Island is now called Iona Island (Figure 11).

It is easy to see why Indian peoples would have occupied Iona Island. Its topography, including rock outcrops with overhanging ledges, provided natural shelters from exposure to the weather and flat, well-drained areas that made excellent open-air campsites. In addition, its proximity to natural resources in the river, the surrounding marsh, and the adjacent forest made it an ideal place for habitation.

The island was then, as it is today, a place of considerable beauty. Throughout the year, the early morning sun would raise mist off the river and direct its warmth onto the island. Bear Mountain to the northwest, West Mountain to the west, and Dunderberg Mountain to the south rise above and surround the island to form a large natural amphitheater. One can easily imagine the sounds of ducks, geese, and other waterfowl intensifying over the low, soft lapping of the rising and falling tidal waters. In the campsites on the island and in adjacent areas, human life would awaken each morning to these melodies, followed by voices, the whispers of paddles cutting through water, and the pleasant smoky smell of wood fires that signaled bands of hunters or travelers coming to life. These early inhabitants recognized the beauty surrounding them as they went about their everyday tasks. The Indians called this place Wanakawaghkin, meaning "pointed land," which probably described the island's position in the river vis-à-vis the land and its geology.

FIGURE II Iona Island (center) and Dunderberg Mountain (right). Photograph by Edward J. Lenik (1995).

IONA ISLAND RIDGE ROCKSHELTER

Trailside staff excavated a large rockshelter located on the spinelike and rugged ridge of Iona Island in 1938. A high overhanging ledge that faces west forms the shelter, creating a small compartment and living area. Several large rock slabs adjacent to the opening provide additional protection from the weather. The entrance is 33 feet wide along its base, 13 feet deep, and about 12–15 feet high. Salisbury Meadow and Snake Hole Creek lie west of the shelter, and the Hudson River is to the east.

Although extensively examined over a period of two days, no cultural features such as hearths were found. The sparse artifact evidence indicates a single, short time occupation by one or two individuals during the Late Woodland period (ca. A.D. 1000–1350). Burggraf found a hammerstone,

FIGURE 12 Restored pottery vessel recovered from the Iona Island Ridge Rockshelter. Photograph by John Korbach. COURTESY PALISADES INTERSTATE PARK COMMISSION.

eight flakes, two bone fragments, and 35 pottery fragments. The pottery fragments were pieced together, producing a nearly complete pot that measures ten inches in height and 6.25 inches in diameter at the shoulder (Figure 12).

Dr. Robert E. Funk, former New York State archaeologist, described the reassembled pot as teardrop in shape with a conoidal base. The lip and upper portion of the pot is decorated with short, oblong-shaped horizontal punctates. These marks occur in a series of wavy rows from the lip of the pot to its shoulder around the vessel. They were probably made by the end of a paddle or stick applied to the soft clay at the time the pot was made. The decoration or pottery type is referred to as Bowman's Brook Incised.

The hammerstone recovered from the Iona Island Ridge Rockshelter, clearly a percussion tool, appears to have a human effigy face on one flat side. This unique feature has special significance because it gives us an indication of the spiritual beliefs and practices of the Indians who occupied this site.

FIGURE 13 A quartzite cobble with an effigy face from the Iona Island Ridge Rockshelter. Photograph by Nancy Gibbs.

The hammerstone is a quartzite cobble, ovoid in shape, and about 2.5 inches across its greatest length. The effigy face consists of two small pits spaced about one inch apart that appear to represent eyes, below which is a vertical rectangular mark or impression that appears to represent a nose (Figure 13). The two pits are natural holes in the stone, but one has been slightly enlarged to provide symmetry. In addition, the edge of the cobble is pecked and forms an outline around the bottom and sides of the face. This pecked outline enhances the face as a whole, and the position of the pits (eyes) and impression (nose) strongly suggests a human visage.

The effigy face is a "Mësingw," or "graven image," and is an indication of Indian spiritual beliefs. It represents a spirit deity, possibly the "Mizinkhalican," meaning "living solid face." According to the anthropologist M. R. Harrington, the Munsee-speaking Lenape or Delaware Indians regarded this important spirit being as a great shaman. It may also have been a means by which an individual made contact with a supernatural power, perhaps the Great Spirit Kishelemukong, the Creator.

A seventeenth-century ethnohistoric account also seems to suggest a spiritual or ceremonial function for effigy faces. In 1650, Adriaen Van der Donck, a Dutch landowner and lawyer living in the Hudson Valley, reported that the dwellings of the Indians, generally those of "chiefs," contained "rough carvings of faces and images."

Two cobbles similar to the one found in the Iona Island Ridge Rockshelter were recovered from the Late Woodland-period Minisink site located in the Upper Delaware River Valley in New Jersey. Each of those specimens also contains an effigy face with a pecked groove around the face. Effigy faces on cobbles, pebbles, pendants, and pottery fragments have been found in widely scattered sites throughout southeastern New York, northern New Jersey, and northeastern Pennsylvania, the former homeland of Munsee-speaking Lenape or Delaware Indians.

THE NAVY ROCKSHELTER

Positioned at the northern end of Iona Island, this site was named for the U.S. Navy ammunition depot that occupied the island between 1900 and 1947. Excavated by Burggraf, it no longer exists, regrettably destroyed by construction probably after 1965 when the park acquired the property.

The Navy Rockshelter has been described as small. Artifacts recovered include two Rossville-type projectile points, one Orient Fishtail point, and one Fox Creek-type point. One flake, one bone fragment, and 230 pottery fragments were also found. The pottery collection contained two rim sherds and about 200 cord-marked body sherds suggesting that the site was occupied during the Terminal Archaic to Early Woodland periods (ca. 2000 B.C. to ca. A.D. 500).

IONA ISLAND ROCKSHELTER NUMBER 25-B

Surrounded by the marsh, this small shelter sits at the base of the ridge, south of the road leading to the island. The overhang faces east and the sheltered area measures 12 feet in width, eight feet in depth, and six feet in height.

Burgraff excavated the shelter in 1939, devoting two days to the work. He reported in his field notes that the site was disturbed. Artifact recoveries were meager and included one hammerstone, three netsinkers, and seven pottery sherds. The presence of pottery within the shelter indicates that Indians occupied it during the Woodland period.

SITE NUMBER 22-B

Burggraf located this site within the south-central section of Iona Island. An open-air campsite, it was minimally excavated in 1935. Artifacts found were a broken projectile point, two scrapers, a "paint stone," and debitage. This evidence is insufficient to make a determination of the site's cultural history. We infer that maintaining tools and processing raw materials took place at this small camp.

IONA ISLAND CAMPSITE

The Iona Island Campsite was discovered in 1990 at the northern end of the island. Artifacts recovered from the surface of the site include a scraper, sinew stone, chert, and jasper debitage. The cultural history and function of this open-air camp have not been determined. The tools and debitage imply that tool production or repair and raw material processing occurred here.

QUARRY

Quartz outcrops lie in the northwestern section of Iona Island. Several ground depressions are present near these sources along with chunks and fragments of quartz. It appears that Indian peoples mined this raw material for making tools.

CHAPTER 5

DUNDERBERG MOUNTAIN AND DOODLETOWN

Dunderberg Mountain rises steeply from the Hudson River until it reaches an elevation of 1,085 feet. This granite massif projects eastward into the river like a giant thumb, creating a sharp bend as the water flows around its base. In the eighteenth century it was called Donder Berg, Dutch for "thunder mountain." Prior to the arrival of Europeans, Indian peoples camped along the base of the mountain and on its several terraces.

DUNDERBERG CAMPSITES

In the 1930s, Burggraff and others discovered and excavated several open-air sites and a rockshelter at the "foot of Dunderberg." Near the river, these sites were easily accessible to Indians traveling by canoe. A small brook flowing down the north slope of the mountain undoubtedly was a source of potable water for the campers. These spots are recorded in Trailside's prehistoric sites inventory as 17-B, 20-B, and 21-B.

Site 17-B consisted of multiple areas: a partially destroyed open-air camp on the south side of the brook; two small, open-air campsites on a level bench about 100 feet above the Hudson to the north of the first site; and scattered traces of occupation on other nearby terraces. Projectile points recovered include triangular forms (Levanna and Madison), Lamoka, Brewerton side-notched, Normanskill, Bare Island, Poplar Island, Susquehanna, Rossville, Fox Creek, and Orient. Other stone tools found were

FIGURE 14 Conjectural scene of a prehistoric Woodland-period camp. Drawing by Tom Fitzpatrick.

scrapers, knives, and pitted hammerstones. Raw materials used to produce these tools included chert (primarily black and gray), quartz, quartzite, argillite, jasper, shale, slate, and sandstone. Debitage, deer bone fragments, and oyster shells were collected as well. Burggraff described the more than 200 pottery fragments found on the campsite on the south side of the brook as being "ornamented," some "net impressed," with sherds from the bottom of a pot "nearly an inch thick." Fragments of deer bone and oyster shells are present within the site collection. The modern Hudson no longer supports oysters, an important staple for the early inhabitants.

This site also contained artifacts dating to the Historic Contact period. These artifacts were European-made ceramics and glass, nails, a pewter spoon, and a fragment of a clay tobacco pipe containing a maker's mark, "R. TIPPETT."

The stone tools, pottery fragments, and Historic Contact material indicate that small groups occupied Site 17-B intermittently over a long span of time, from 4000 B.C. to about A.D. 1750. They also suggest that hunting, food processing and consumption, and tool making and repair activities occurred at this locale.

Site 21-B, also known as Dunderberg Site 2, sat on a narrow terrace overlooking the small brook to the south and the Hudson River to the east. Burggraff extensively excavated this campsite, but no excavation records are on file. In a letter to the archaeologist William A. Ritchie, dated November 1, 1944, Burggraf wrote of 21-B:

> The soil must be too acid to preserve any bone or shell and there were no refuse pits to provide sufficient alkaline concentrations to overcome the sour soils' corrosive action. I think the site was a hunting camp, a base from which the Indians could cover the fine deer forest surrounding the present Iona Island swamp with a strategic gully running up the almost precipitous slopes of Dunderberg providing a fairly easy trail to the flat summit. . . . The cove on the Hudson provided a sheltered beach for their dugouts and a never failing spring run assured ice cold pure water at all times.

Sixty-nine projectile points were recovered including such types as Bare Island, Vosburg, Brewerton side-notched, Brewerton eared, Lamoka, Susquehanna, Snook Kill, Perkiomen, Poplar Island, Adena,

Levanna, and Madison. Other items found were a celt, an ax, a muller, a fragmentary spear-thrower (atlatl) weight, hammerstones, scrapers, bifaces, and a broken pendant or gorget. Some 50 fragments of pottery were recovered, along with trade goods that date to the Historic Contact period, namely a gunflint, a brass thimble, and two brass buttons.

The evidence from 21-B indicates that the campsite was occupied intermittently from the Late Archaic period to the Historic Contact period. The data suggests it was used as a hunting and travel camp by small groups of people (Figure 14). The presence of woodworking tools (ax and celt), scrapers, and hammerstones indicates that raw material processing took place some time.

Rockshelter Site 20-B was located on the north side of the brook. No record of the actual excavation has been found, but Trailside's artifact inventory suggests that the rockshelter was excavated extensively. The collection includes Brewerton side-notched, Normanskill, Bare Island, Rossville, Green, and Levanna projectile points. Two scrapers, bifaces, debitage, and 50 net-impressed pottery fragments make up the balance of the collection. This implies that the shelter was occupied during Late Archaic and Woodland times. In 1944, Burggraf speculated that the rockshelter "could have been inhabited" by the same "band" of Indians who occupied nearby Site 17-B.

MOLLY BAKER'S ROCK ROCKSHELTER

Near the northwest side of Dunderberg Mountain is a rock outcrop or knob known as Molly Baker's Rock. Local folklore states that this place was named for a woman who was allegedly murdered by her husband on Old Route 9W prior to the 1930s.

In 1936, Burggraf and Trailside's historian, Richard Koke, discovered and excavated a small rockshelter on the west side of Molly Baker's Rock. Their field notes indicate that the shelter was nine feet wide, five feet deep, and four feet high.

Artifacts were sparse. A projectile point recovered from the site has the following morphological characteristics: The blade has convex sides, a tapering stem, and was finely made from purple argillite. This unusual point style does not resemble the projectile-point types commonly found in New York; it resembles the Neville Stemmed point, which was first recognized as a type in New England and probably dates to the Middle to Late Archaic period.

A pebble hammerstone and two chert spalls were recovered from the site. In 2002, a large hammerstone was found on the ground just outside the shelter. Its size and battered end suggest that it was used for heavy-duty percussion work.

AYERS HOUSE CAMPSITE

The Ayers House was located on the southeastern slope of Dunderberg Mountain in the area formerly called Caldwell's Landing, now known as Jones Point. The 1876 map of Stony Point Township indicates that the house was occupied by "T. Ayers" and was situated on the northwest side of the Caldwell Turnpike, now called Old Route 9W.

The Indian camp was located about 100 feet up the slope of the mountain. Field notes at Trailside indicate that broken projectile points collected from the surface of the house and garden site were donated to the museum in 1939. No other details are given, so we infer that this was an open-air campsite. Unfortunately, the artifact collection has been lost, and we are unable to determine the cultural history and nature of this site.

DOODLETOWN

The historic hamlet of Doodletown lays in a picturesque mountain valley between Bear Mountain to the north and Bald and Dunderberg mountains to the south. Doodletown Brook—once known by its Indian name Tongapogh Kil, meaning "little rock"—flows easterly through the hamlet and enters the Hudson near Iona Island. The deep and brooding valley sits high above the Iona marsh, providing refuge, shelter, and an inland alternative for camping and travel.

The first colonial settlers in the valley were Ithiel June Jr. and his wife, Charity (Baxter) June, who moved here in the early 1760s. Others soon followed, and by the early twentieth century they had established a hamlet of some 75 people. Most residents were farmers, woodcutters, and iron miners. By 1945 about 300 people lived in Doodletown. By the mid-1960s, the Park Commission had acquired all of the land and structures within the hamlet and had the homes and outbuildings demolished.

Indian people lived in Doodletown long before the arrival of the settlers. Archaeological evidence suggests that a few individuals lived here well into the Historic period. The habitations of Indians were discovered and investigated during the first half of the twentieth century.

THE DOODLETOWN (JUNE'S) ROCKHOUSE

The Doodletown Rockhouse sits on a level terrace within the former hamlet, surrounded by rugged mountainous terrain. The shelter is formed by a large rock slab that leans at an angle against an enormous boulder forming an interior space 21 feet deep, 6.5 feet wide, and six feet high. Its opening faces northwest (Figure 15).

Indians were drawn to the site by three principal factors: First, the rock provided excellent protection from the elements. Second, Doodletown Brook was a readily available source of fresh water for the site's occupants. Third, abundant flora and fauna existed in the adjacent mountains and along the Iona marsh and Hudson River to the east.

Max Schrabisch excavated the Doodletown Rockhouse at some time before 1936 (Figure 16). He called it "June's Rock" because supposedly a man of Indian ancestry named June occupied it "about a century ago."

In 1936, Schrabisch reported that the ground surface within the shelter contained "fragments of crockery . . . iron nails . . . also a few chips of chert, quartz and slate." At a depth of four to seven inches below the surface, he recovered the bases of two large blades, a projectile-point fragment, nine chert flakes, and four quartzite nodules. In the center of the shelter, Schrabisch found evidence of a fire hearth as indicated by the presence of charcoal mixed into the soil. Schrabisch concluded that the site had few visitors and that the lack of pottery fragments and bones suggested that the shelter was used as a workshop.

In 1938, Burggraf re-excavated the entire interior of the shelter and the flat living floor area outside the entrance. He recovered one Poplar Island point; one untyped point with a contracting stem, narrow blade, and barbs; one triangular point made from quartz; a large green chert flake that was used as a side scraper; two chert scrapers; one quartzite scraper; hammerstones; pestle fragments; a piece of shell; and several decorated pottery fragments dating to the Late Woodland period. Two whiteware ceramic fragments and a mule shoe from the Historic period were also found.

The presence of stemmed projectile points, the triangular point, and the decorated potsherds suggest that the site was occupied during the Late Archaic and Late Woodland periods.

FIGURE 15 The Doodletown Rockshelter. Photograph by Edward J. Lenik (1995).

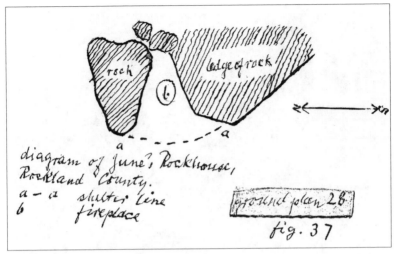

FIGURE 16 Plan of Doodletown (June's) Rockhouse by Max Schrabisch. DRAWING COURTESY NEW YORK STATE MUSEUM.

OTHER CAMPSITES WITHIN DOODLETOWN

Burggraf and John Kenney, director of the Trailside Museums, archaeologically tested a high terrace south of Doodletown Brook in 1939. Their field notes indicate that only debitage was found here.

In 1935, Burggraf reported finding a quartz scraper and several white quartz flakes "some distance west" of Luke Stalter's house. The data from this and the previously mentioned site are insufficient to determine the cultural history of these campsites.

Trailside's prehistoric artifact collections include 218 pottery fragments recovered from an undescribed site at Doodletown. This unknown site, designated 28-B in the inventory records, dates to the Woodland period of Indian cultural history.

RETROSPECT AND PROSPECT

W hat follows is a summary of the surveys and excavations conducted within Bear Mountain State Park over the past 70 years. It considers the implications of the data previously presented for locational selectivity, cultural chronology, lithic technology and tool use, and site functions. The role and placement of the Bear Mountain sites in the regional settlement pattern of Indian peoples is also examined.

LOCATIONAL SELECTIVITY ANALYSIS

The major Indian occupation zones located in the park can be divided into three basic site types: rockshelters, stream and river camps, and elevated terraces.

Geology, topography, and soil were of primary importance to Indian peoples when considering where to camp and live. The geology of the area consists of Precambrian bedrock overlaid with unconsolidated deposits left behind by the retreat of the last glacier in the Wisconsin period. The presence of great masses of exposed bedrock and depositional material, such as boulders, precluded Indian occupation in many areas. Significant amounts of rock-covered land surface would have made many areas unsuitable. The Indians, however, used rockshelters, or ledge-like rock overhangs of bedrock or large boulders, as shelters and campsites.

Wide variations in topography exist within the park, many offering attractive locations for occupation. Although the terrain is difficult and the slopes steep, several flat terraces or benches that overlook the creeks, brooks, and Hudson River occur throughout the area. These terraces and benches provided excellent strategic locations for campsites, accessible yet protected with good views of surrounding riverine areas where potential food animals might gather to drink. Narrow, flat strips of land just above the Hudson were also used because of their proximity to potable water, aquatic food, and raw materials (Figure 17).

Diverse terrestrial and aquatic environments in the region undoubtedly played a role in the selection of a place to camp. The woodlands, marsh, lake, streams, and river yielded a large variety of floral and faunal resources for use as food and other subsistence needs. The range of aquatic and terrestrial fauna was enormous: hundreds of species of large and small mammals, reptiles and amphibians, fish and shellfish, as well as migratory and non-migratory birds would have provided a plentiful supply of food for native peoples. Unfortunately, archaeological evidence for the use of faunal resources at the sites investigated is meager.

Regional botanic environments are equally diverse. Numerous species of plants and shrubs could be gathered and processed for food, medicine, or other utilitarian purposes. Commonly exploited edible plant products such as nuts and berries were abundant. Some of the plants used as medicinals were ladyslipper; jewelweed; burdock; the bark of tulip and butternut or white walnut trees; also sassafras, which was used as an eye tonic and for tea; and spotted wintergreen, used by the Delaware Indians in the Historic period as a treatment for cystitis, rheumatism, stomach problems, and kidney infections. No evidence of any floral species has been found in the park's archaeological record, undoubtedly due to the highly acidic soils in the region and the lack of effort and means to recover floral specimens by archaeologists.

FIGURE 17 A winter camp in the forest. DRAWING COURTESY DAVID R. WAGNER.

CULTURAL CHRONOLOGY: THE TYPOLOGICAL EVIDENCE

The age of the sites in this study was determined by the presence of diagnostic artifacts such as stone tools and pottery fragments since no radiocarbon dates were secured from any of the sites. The most common class of tools collected was that of projectile points. Those points that could be typed are dated by the previously defined cultural manifestations that occurred in the area and by the typology developed by former New York State Archaeologist William Ritchie.

The artifacts indicate that the Bear Mountain area was occupied intermittently from the Late Archaic period up to and including the Historic Contact period, ca. 4000 B.C. to ca. A.D. 1750. The archaeological record suggests an intense period of occupation during the Late Archaic period, as shown by the abundance of such projectile-point types as Vosburg, Brewerton, Normanskill, Otter Creek, Bare Island, Poplar Island, and Lamoka.

Traces of occupation during the Terminal Archaic and Early Woodland periods were also found, as indicated by projectile-point types such as Orient Fishtail, Snook Kill, Fox Creek, Rossville, Susquehanna, Adena, and Meadowood. The Vinette 1-type pot recovered from the Bear Mountain Railroad Station Rockshelter also dates to the Early Woodland period.

Artifacts of the Middle to Late Woodland periods (ca. A.D. 1–1500) were common and indicate frequent occupation by Indians during that time. The artifacts recovered include Levanna- and Madison-type projectile points and a partially restored Bowman's Brook-type pot found in the Iona Island Rockshelter.

Evidence of Indian occupation during the Historic Contact period (ca. A.D. 1524–1750) was found at four sites: a glass trade bead from an eighteenth-century deposit located east of the Fort Clinton Prehistoric Site; a log bowl from Hessian Lake; European-made ceramics, glass, nails, pewter spoons, and a clay tobacco pipe from the Dunderberg campsite; and a triangular-shaped arrowhead made of brass from the site of the one-story barracks at Fort Montgomery. Although these finds are meager, they nevertheless indicate the presence of Indian people in this portion of the Hudson Valley during early historic times.

LITHIC TECHNOLOGY AND TOOL USE

The vast majority of artifactual material consisted of stone tools and debitage. The raw materials from which the tools were manufactured are found in the glacial till that occurs throughout the region in pebble or cobble form. Cobbles consisting of quartz, quartzite, and various grades of black, gray, and brown cherts are present. Quartz veins occur in the gneissic bedrock at several nearby locations, and at least one of these primary sources, on Iona Island, appears to have been exploited by Indian peoples.

Bear Mountain had an abundance of life-sustaining resources. Tools were needed to procure and facilitate manipulation of these resources. Native peoples used a variety of raw lithic materials from which they formed their projectile points, knives, scrapers, axes, hammerstones, netsinkers, drills, and other specialized processing tools. At Bear Mountain, black and gray colored cherts, of variable shades, were the predominant raw materials used in making projectile points. Other frequently used materials were quartz, quartzite, shale, argillite, and jasper. The presence of small amounts of jasper, a so-called exotic material, was found at the Fort Montgomery and Fort Clinton campsites. The nearest primary sources of jasper occur in Pennsylvania and Rhode Island. However, pebbles and cobbles of jasper may be found locally. Hence, the presence of jasper may reflect glacial transport or human transport or trade obtained from known outcrops many miles away.

The analysis of the stone tools and debitage recovered from the various sites indicates that all stages of tool manufacture, as well as tool maintenance and repair, took place. The artifact collections contain cortical fragments and flakes (from cobbles); tertiary, thinning and retouch flakes; cores, blanks, and preforms.

The debitage suggests the following steps in producing tools (projectile points, knives, scrapers): the knapper found cobbles of chert on the surface of terraces or along the banks of nearby streams; the knapper delivered a blow to the cobble with a hammerstone to detach a large flake; the knapper used harder hammer blows to remove additional primary and secondary cortical flakes from the core. This operation also produced irregularly shaped fragments or shatter; large flakes and fragments were bifacially reduced by percussion to form facial surfaces of tool-blade preforms; the blanks or preforms were further reduced by trimming and thinning the edge with an antler pressure-flaking tool.

A function analysis of the tools that were found gives us some insight into the subsistence activities that took place here. By definition, projectile points are bifacially worked stone points that are attached to a shaft (spear or arrow) and are presumed to have been made for the primary purpose of hunting—that is, the spearing or shooting of prey. Projectile points, both whole and broken, were the most common tools found in the area. The presence of broken points suggests that some of them may have been used for purposes other than hunting, such as cutting, scraping, or prying, and became broken or dulled as a result of these processes and were discarded. A few knives and scrapers were also found that were probably used to cut or draw over such material as hides, wood, bone, or antler.

Hammerstones were found at Fort Clinton, Fort Montgomery, two Dunderberg sites, the Molly Baker's and Doodletown rockshelters, and two rockshelters on Iona Island. These specimens are clearly percussion tools. A cobble-type sinker was found at Fort Montgomery, and a pebble netsinker was found at the Iona Island rockshelter. These specimens suggest that some type of fishing activity took place at these sites.

In summary, the functional range of stone tools that were found in the area is very limited. The majority of the tools are related to the procurement and processing of locally available flora and fauna, while the hammerstones are related to tool manufacturing itself. The presence of pottery sherds at nearly all of the sites described indicates that food was prepared and consumed at these sites.

BEAR MOUNTAIN SITES IN A REGIONAL CONTEXT

The Hudson Valley region surrounding Bear Mountain State Park is rich in evidence of Native American occupations. In particular, sites near the Hudson River, adjacent rivers and streams, and rockshelters in mountainous and hilly areas have long been identified as places where Indians lived and worked. The archaeological and historical evidence indicates that several types of sites are present in the region, including villages, base camps, procurement and processing camps, travel camps, rockshelters, burial sites, shell middens, lithic scatters, and workshops and quarries. These sites occupy a variety of geophysical settings such as flood plains, valley terraces and side slopes, marshes or wetlands, and hilltops.

The artifactual assemblage from sites in the region indicates that all cultural-historic periods from the Paleo Indian era to the Historic Contact period are represented in the region. Many of these sites were repeatedly revisited throughout the prehistoric era, while others were single-occupation sites.

Two types of sites are in evidence within Bear Mountain: rockshelters and campsites on terraces or benches. As with other sites in the region, some Bear Mountain locales were heavily used, while others show evidence of a single visit. The occupation of these sites seems to have been temporary or short term in nature and focused primarily on the procurement and processing of subsistence resources and raw materials. The limited range and diversity of artifactual material from these sites, as well as the lack of evidence for intense or long-term occupation, indicate that they were utilized by small groups of Indians as transient campsites or as small procurement camps at various times during the Late Archaic to Historic Contact periods. The subsistence and settlement patterns here are consistent with those found within rockshelters and campsites in the entire Hudson Valley region. The Bear Mountain State Park sites are part of a network of temporarily occupied sites that were related to a hunting and gathering subsistence economy that was practiced in this region throughout all cultural periods.

PROSPECT AND RESEARCH DIRECTIONS

The discovery, identification, and preservation of Indian sites and artifacts in the Park was a pioneering effort in the region. The Park's staff, with minimal funding and few hands, located and excavated a remarkable number of sites in Bear Mountain and Harriman state parks. Some 70 Indian sites of various types and in various settings were investigated and documented. Many of the artifacts and several of the sites have been incorporated into exhibits in the Historical Museum at Trailside. They present a wonderful picture of Native American culture history and lifeways in the parks.

The field notes, artifacts, artifact inventories, analyses, notes, and some photographs pertaining to the various sites are all preserved in a research facility on Iona Island. These materials are a treasure trove of information that has yet to be mined. Much more can be learned from the excavated material. For example, the collections contain faunal material, primarily bone fragments, which need to be analyzed to determine the type of animals sought, procured, and consumed by Indian peoples at the various sites. In addition to taxonomic identification, the age, sex, relative size, and season of death of the various specimens can yield important clues about hunting methods, social organization, seasonal cycles, and technology. There is also a need for future lithic research. Since it appears that chert pebbles and cobbles were used extensively to make tools in the region, it would be interesting to know the knapping quality of these various cobble materials found in the region and to construct a pebble lithology for the area. Pottery fragments were found at many sites, and these specimens need to be analyzed to determine method of manufacture, tempering material used, sources of clay, vessel attributes such as surface treatment and decorative techniques, and minimal vessel counts.

In sum, the potential for extracting additional information on Native American lifeways and use of park landforms from the previous archaeological excavations and artifact collections has not yet been reached.

EPILOGUE

PROTECTING OUR HERITAGE

B ear Mountain and Harriman state parks were the focus of extensive and intensive land use by Indian peoples for more than 10,000 years. By 1683, Dutch settlers had begun to acquire land in the region from the Indians. Following these land transactions, the Dutch, and later the English, began to settle in this section of the Hudson Valley.

Evidence of Indian occupation and the later historic-period land-use activities exists in many forms within the parks. It includes such features as rockshelters, open-air campsites, cellar holes and foundations, mines, and prehistoric and historic archaeological materials. This body of evidence is a heritage resource recognized by the parks' administration and researched, interpreted, and protected by the staff and volunteers of the Trailside Museums.

The Indian and historic-period archaeological sites are nonrenewable cultural resources. Unlike plants and wildlife, cultural resources once destroyed cannot be replaced. Unfortunately, some of the sites in the parks are being vandalized and otherwise harmed by careless hikers, litterbugs, and artifact hunters.

To counter such activities, Jack Focht, former director of the Trailside Museums, and I developed and implemented a Heritage Site Steward Program for Bear Mountain and Harriman state parks in 1998. Volunteers from environmental organizations and hiking clubs, together with park staff, are now monitoring the condition of the archaeological sites to help preserve them by preventing the illegal activity of digging for artifacts and to educate the public about preserving such sites.

HELP US PRESERVE OUR CULTURAL AND NATURAL RESOURCES.

GLOSSARY

ABRADING STONES: Granular abrasive rocks used to polish, grind, sharpen, and shape stone tools, bone awls, antler tools, and wood.

ANVIL STONE: A cobble, block of stone, slab, or bedrock surface that shows irregular but concentrated nicks or pits. The nicks or pits were produced by percussion. The anvil stones may have served in bipolar stone tool manufacturing or in the processing of food.

ARGILLITE: Metamorphosed siliceous rock composed of compacted clay or silty particles.

ARTIFACT: Any material that has been modified or produced by humans.

ASSEMBLAGE: A collection of artifacts that comes from a specific site, area, or cultural component, or that shares certain physical attributes.

ATLATL WEIGHTS: A stone weight fastened to a throwing board or spearthrower; formerly called bannerstones.

BASALT: Fine-grained, dark-colored volcanic rock.

BIFACE: This class of artifacts represents pieces of stone that have been flaked on both sides. It may represent a tool that was in the process of being manufactured.

BLANK: Lithic material in the form of a flat tabular blade, or squared or columnar, that has the potential to enter the bifacial-tool-reduction sequence.

CELT: A wedge-shaped ground or polished stone tool used as an ax.

CHERT: Compact, opaque to slightly translucent, microcrystalline silica rock.

CORES: Stones that serve as parent material from which pieces have been flaked off to make artifacts.

CORTEX: The weathered, smooth exterior surface of stone. The presence of cortex on an artifact is usually an indicator of an early stage of manufacture.

DEBITAGE: The discarded pieces of stone from tool manufacturing or refurbishing activities. Commonly referred to as flakes, chips, scatter, or fragments.

FEATURE: A soil disturbance or discoloration produced by human activity or an artifact that is too large or impractical to remove from a site—for example, fire hearths, storage pits, or post molds.

FLAKE: A piece of waste material from the manufacture of stone tools created by percussion or pressure applied by an object such as a hammerstone, antler flaker, or billet.

> **BIFACIAL THINNING FLAKE:** Thin, flat, small flake, less than 20 mm long.

> **PRESSURE OR RETOUCH FLAKE:** Tiny or very small flake less than 10 mm long, with flat or convex cross-sections.

> **PRIMARY CORTICAL FLAKE:** Flake with more than 50 percent of cortex remaining on its outer surface.

> **SECONDARY CORTICAL FLAKE:** Usually wide and long flake, thick in cross-section. Less than 50 percent of cortex present.

TERTIARY FLAKE: Long, broad, thin flake; multiple flake scars on outer surfaces and small bulbs of percussion.

GORGET: A thin, usually rectangular stone artifact with two drilled holes for suspension. For personal adornment, worn at the breast.

HAMMERSTONE: A hand-held or hafted stone used as a hammer. It has a variety of forms and shows evidence of battering in one or more areas.

LITHIC: An object made of stone.

MULLER: A small, flat-faced cobblestone used for grinding.

NODULE: Rounded, irregularly shaped mineral stone such as chert. Used in making a stone tool.

PREFORM: A piece of stone that has been flaked and shaped to a symmetrical outline. It may be four-sided, triangular, or oval, with a regular lensatic cross-section.

PROJECTILE POINT: A bifacially flaked tool having one end pointed and the opposite modified for hafting. This term includes tools that have been used as hunting implements (arrowheads or spear points) or knives.

QUARRY: A place where stones are dug from the earth (stream bed, gravel bank) or where stone is removed from veins, pockets, or exposed rock faces.

SCRAPER: A bifacially or unifacially flaked tool with an angled working edge used for scraping hides, bone, wood, and other materials.

SHATTER: Irregular fragments of stone discarded during tool manufacture.

SHERD: A fragment of broken pottery.

SPALL: A stone chip produced through natural forces or by the force of a hammer blow.

STRATIGRAPHY: Natural or cultural soil layers in an archaeological site.

UTILIZED FLAKE: A waste flake with a dulled or damaged edge indicating that it has been used as an expedient tool.

BIBLIOGRAPHY

Brawer, Catherine C.

1983   *Many Trails, Indians of the Lower Hudson Valley.*
        Katonah Gallery, Katonah, NY.

Budke, George H. (compiler)

1975   *Indian Deeds, 1630 to 1748.* Reprinted by the Library
        Association of Rockland County, New City, NY.

Burggraf, James D.

n.d.   "Bear Mountain Historical Museum. Contacts—Indian
        and Historical." Typed report. On file at Trailside Muse-
        ums, Palisades Interstate Park, Bear Mountain, NY.

1943   Letter, February 19, New York Central Railroad Camp,
        Iona Island, NY, to Archaeologist William A. Ritchie.
        On file at Trailside Museums, Palisades Interstate Park,
        Bear Mountain, NY.

[1943?] Letter, October 20, New York Central Railroad Camp,
        Iona Island, NY, to Archaeologist William A. Ritchie.
        On file at Trailside Museums, Palisades Interstate Park,
        Bear Mountain, NY.

1944   Letter, November 1, Samsonville, NY, to Archaeologist
        William A. Ritchie. On file at Trailside Museums,
        Palisades Interstate Park, Bear Mountain, NY.

1990   "Indian Pot Found at Bear Mountain." Trailside Museums
        & Zoo Historical Papers, #H-15/90. Palisades Interstate
        Park Commission, Bear Mountain, NY.

Carr, William H.

1937   *Ten Years of Nature Trailing: The Nature Trails and Trailside Museums at Bear Mountain, New York*. Department of Education, American Museum of Natural History, New York.

Eager, Samuel W.

1846–47   *An Outline History of Orange County*. S.T. Callahan, Newburgh, NY.

Funk, Robert E.

1976   *Recent Contributions to Hudson Valley Prehistory*. New York State Museum and Science Service Memoir 22. Albany, NY.

Goddard, Ives

1978   "Delaware." In *Handbook of North American Indians*, edited by W. C. Sturtevant, vol. 15, pp. 213–239. Smithsonian Institution, Washington, DC.

1978   "Eastern Algonkian Languages." In *Handbook of North American Indians*, edited by W. C. Sturtevant, vol. 15, pp. 10–77. Smithsonian Institution, Washington, DC.

Harrington, M. R.

1921   "Religion and Ceremonies of the Lenape." *Indian Notes and Monographs*, 2nd series, vol. 19. Museum of the American Indian, Heye Foundation, New York.

Kidd, Kenneth E., and Martha Ann Kidd

1970   "A Classification System for Glass Beads for the Use of Field Archaeologists" *Canadian Historic Sites: Occasional Papers in Archaeology and History*, No 1. National Historic Sites Service, Ottawa, Ontario, Canada.

Koke, Richard J., and James D. Burggraf

1937   "Fort Clinton in the Highlands of the Hudson: Report of the Bear Mountain Trailside Museum 1935–1936." Manuscript. Copy on file at Trailside Museums, Palisades Interstate Park, Bear Mountain, NY.

Kraft, Herbert C.

1986   *The Lenape. Archaeology, History and Ethnography.*
New Jersey Historical Society, Newark, NJ.

Lenik, Edward J.

1991   "Patterns of Lithic Resource Selection in the Highlands
Region of Northern New Jersey and Southeastern New
York." *Bulletin of the Archaeological Society of New Jersey* 46:
13–17.

1995   "A Log Bowl from Hessian Lake." Trailside Museums
Historical Papers #H-4/95. Palisades Interstate Park
Commission, Bear Mountain, NY.

1999   *Indians in the Ramapos.* North Jersey Highlands Historical
Society, Ringwood, NJ.

Lenik, Edward J., and Diane Dallal

1992   *Stage I and II Archaeological Investigations for Service Access
Improvements on the Site of Fort Clinton, Trailside Museums,
Palisades Interstate Park, Bear Mountain, New York.*
Sheffield Archaeological Consultants, Butler, NJ.

Megapolensis Jr., Johannes (Reverend)

1644   "A Short Account of the Mohawk Indians, 1644."
In *Narratives of New Netherland 1609–1664*, edited
by Franklin Jameson. Barnes and Noble, New York.

Myles, William J.

1992   *Harriman Trails. A Guide and History.* New York–
New Jersey Trail Conference, New York.

Palisades Interstate Park Commission

1996   "Inventory of Prehistoric Sites within Bear Mountain,
Harriman, Goosepond, and Rockland Lake New York
State Parks." Summary inventory prepared by Sheffield
Archaeological Consultants, Butler, NJ.

Ritchie, William A.

1971   *A Typology and Nomenclature for New York Projectile Points.*
        Revised. New York State Museum and Science Service,
        Bulletin 384, Albany, NY.

Ruttenber, E. M.

1872   *History of the Indian Tribes of Hudson's River.* Kennikat Press,
        Port Washington, NY.

Salomon, Julian H.

1982   *Indians of the Lower Hudson Region: The Munsee.*
        Historical Society of Rockland County, New City, NY.

Schrabisch, Max

1936   *The Archaeology of Southern New York.* Unpublished manu-
        script. On file at New York State Museum, Albany, NY.

Stalter, Elizabeth

1996   *Doodletown. Hiking through History in a Vanished Hamlet on
        the Hudson.* Palisades Interstate Park Commission Press,
        Bear Mountain, NY.

Tedesco-Talamini, Joann

1995   Transcript describing the recovery of a log bowl from
        Hessian Lake, dated March 14. On file at Trailside
        Museums, Palisades Interstate Park, Bear Mountain, NY.

Van der Donck, Adriaen

1650   "The Representation of New Netherland 1650."
        In *Narratives of New Netherland, 1609–1664*, edited
        by J. Franklin Jameson, pp. 67–69. Barnes and Noble,
        New York.

Whritenour, Raymond

2002   Personal communication. Lenape Texts and Studies,
        Butler, NJ.

NATIVE AMERICAN SITE
STEWARD PROGRAM

N ative Americans within Harriman and Bear Mountain state parks date back thousands of years, representing many generations of indigenous peoples. Evidence of these people can be found in artifacts left behind, such as those you see in this book.

Unfortunately, looting and other illegal activities threaten the condition of these irreplaceable cultural resources. In 1998, Jack Focht, former director of Trailside, and Edward J. Lenik, consultant archaeologist, devised a program to aid in protecting this heritage.

The Native American Site Steward Program consists of volunteers who routinely check these sites as their mission:

> ➤ To preserve prehistoric and historic archaeological resources for conservation, scientific study, and interpretation

> ➤ To increase public awareness of the significance and value of cultural resources and the damage done by artifact hunters, collectors, uninformed hikers, and day campers, and

> ➤ To discourage vandalism of Native American sites.

The NASSP is an essential step in preserving the Hudson Highlands' past for the future.

For more information on becoming involved, please inquire at the Trailside office: (845) 786-2701 ext. 265.

NOTICE

NATIVE AMERICAN CAMPSITES ARE FRAGILE

AND IRREPLACEABLE HERITAGE RESOURCES.

HUMAN OCCUPATION IN THIS AREA

DATES BACK TO AT LEAST 5000 B.C.

DIGGING FOR ARTIFACTS IN THE PARK IS ILLEGAL.

VIOLATORS WILL BE PROSECUTED.

ILLEGAL DIGGING DESTROYS THE HERITAGE

OF NATIVE PEOPLE AND SCIENTIFIC

INFORMATION ABOUT PAST CULTURES.

PLEASE HELP US MAKE SURE THAT

NEW YORK'S PAST HAS A FUTURE.

REPORT ANY ACTIVITIES THAT THREATEN

OUR CULTURAL AND NATURAL RESOURCES TO

THE STATE PARK POLICE OR PARK RANGERS:

(845) 786-2781.

THANK YOU!